OHIO   STUDIES   IN   PERSONNEL

Methods in the Study of Administrative Leadership

By
Ralph M. Stogdill
and
Carroll L. Shartle

RESEARCH   MONOGRAPH   NUMBER   80
BUREAU   OF   BUSINESS   RESEARCH
THE   OHIO   STATE   UNIVERSITY

METHODS IN THE STUDY OF ADMINISTRATIVE LEADERSHIP

Date Loaned

METHODS IN THE STUDY OF ADMINISTRATIVE LEADERSHIP

By

Ralph M. Stogdill

and

Carroll L. Shartle

Published by

**BUREAU OF BUSINESS RESEARCH
COLLEGE OF COMMERCE AND ADMINISTRATION
THE OHIO STATE UNIVERSITY
COLUMBUS 10, OHIO**

unacc.

COLLEGE OF COMMERCE AND ADMINISTRATION

WALTER C. WEIDLER, *Dean*

BUREAU OF BUSINESS RESEARCH STAFF

VIVA BOOTHE, *Director*

ALTON W. BAKER, *Personnel* MIKHAIL V. CONDOIDE, *Economics*
(On Leave, 1954–55)

JAMES C. YOCUM, *Marketing*

RALPH M. STOGDILL, *Research Associate*

OMAR GOODE, *Tabulations*

Research Assistants

EYVONNE COCHRAN	MARTHA N. STRATTON
PAUL CRAIG	RIMMER DE VRIES
MARY PRIEST MARTIN	CAROL G. WILSON

MARTHA MOUNTS, *Assistant to the Director*

THE OHIO STATE UNIVERSITY

PERSONNEL RESEARCH BOARD

FREDERICK W. HEIMBERGER, *Vice President of the University*, Chairman
CARROLL L. SHARTLE, *Professor of Psychology*, Executive Director
EDMUND D. AYRES, *Professor of Electrical Engineering*
VIVA BOOTHE, *Director, Bureau of Business Research*
EDISON L. BOWERS, *Chairman, Department of Economics*
HAROLD E. BURTT, *Chairman, Department of Psychology*
GORDON B. CARSON, *Dean, College of Engineering*
DONALD P. COTTRELL, *Dean, College of Education*
RALPH L. DEWEY, *Professor of Economics*
HAROLD P. FAWCETT, *Chairman, Department of Education*
ARTHUR W. FOSHAY, *Director, Bureau of Educational Research*
ROBERT S. GREEN, *Director, Engineering Experiment Station*
MICHAEL J. JUCIUS, *Professor of Business Organization*
PAUL N. LEHOCZKY, *Chairman, Department of Industrial Engineering*
HAROLD H. MAYNARD, *Chairman, Department of Business Organization*
RAYMOND F. SLETTO, *Chairman, Department of Sociology and Anthropology*
WALTER C. WEIDLER, *Dean, College of Commerce and Administration*

FOREWORD

The methods reported in this monograph were designed for the study of leadership in terms of the status, interactions, perceptions and behavior of individuals in relation to other members of the organized group. Thus, leadership is regarded as a relationship between persons rather than as a characteristic of the isolated individual. When the data for all the members of a group collected by these methods are combined and interrelated, they provide a means of studying leadership in terms of the structural and functional dimensions of organization. The methods may then be regarded as representing modified forms of position analysis and of organization analysis. It is one of the distinctive features of the research in which these methods are used that leadership is regarded not only in terms of the individual but also in terms of the organization as a whole.

Data are presented relative to the reliability and validity of the various methods. However, the authors advise that the methods be used only for purposes of research. They have wisely cautioned that it will be necessary to accumulate data on a wide variety of organizations under varying conditions of demand and operations before valid norms can be established for the evaluation of administrative performance.

A list of the studies, with a short descriptive statement concerning each, in which these methods have been used is given in Appendix A.

This monograph is one of the Ohio Studies in Personnel published by the Bureau of Business Research as a part of the program of the Personnel Research Board.

VIVA BOOTHE, *Director*
The Bureau of Business Research

PREFACE

The Ohio State Leadership Studies were initiated in 1945 by the Personnel Research Board. They were designed as a ten-year program of basic research with the aims of developing research methods and of obtaining information which might lead to a better understanding of leadership. Practical aims were also kept in mind as secondary objectives. For example, it was hoped that the research might produce data which would eventually be of value in the selection, training and assignment of persons for leadership roles.

The research to date has been largely confined to business, educational and military organizations. Some work has been done on the subject of leadership in experimentally created groups. However, most of the studies have been concerned with subjects whose leadership status was already established. Business executives, college administrators, school superintendents, aircraft commanders and Navy officers have been studied.

One of the primary aims of the research was the development of methodology. It was decided at the outset to make a marked departure from traditional methods, not because there is any merit in meaningless innovation, but because theoretical and methodological developments in industrial psychology and social psychology were pointing the way toward a new approach to the study of leadership. Leadership was no longer being regarded as a characteristic of isolated individuals. It was being viewed instead as a relationship among the members of a social group.

In planning the studies, it was realized that social scientists differ in their opinions about the "right" way to conduct a study of leadership. The idea that there is only one right way was rejected as injurious to scientific progress. It was believed that an interdisciplinary approach would broaden the field of inquiry, and that the utilization of both practitioners and theorists as consultants would serve to keep the research oriented toward everyday realities. Morris and Seeman have described some of the thinking of the staff relative to the scope of the leadership problem.

The scientists selected to carry out the research were economists, psychologists and sociologists. In order to preserve the right to freedom of scientific inquiry, each project director was given complete freedom, subject to the pressure of staff opinion, to follow the line of inquiry and to develop the methodologies which he regarded as most useful for the research tasks to be undertaken. The result has been a variety of approaches to the study of leadership. Studies have been made in the areas of business leadership, educational leadership, air force leadership and naval leadership. A brief description of these studies is given below.

Groups usually organize for the purpose of creating some value for the members and, often, for the public in general. Coons made a study of wholesale cooperative associations, with special attention to the relation of leadership to the economic and social values accruing from cooperative enterprise. His study was a longitudinal one, covering changes in leadership, organization structure, economic growth and cooperative philosophy. Changes in leadership style were apparent at different stages in the growth of the cooperative movement.

Fleishman studied the results of a training course upon the leader behavior of foremen in a manufacturing plant. He found that the behavior of the foremen in their jobs after attending a training course is related to the leadership climate created by their superiors in the organization.

Each member of an organization is also a member of a larger social order, including the community in which he lives and the other organizations to which he belongs. He holds some more or less well-defined status in the community and incorporates attitudes and ideologies which are derived from the total environmental *milieu* in which the organization operates. Seeman has conducted studies of public school superintendents, principals and teachers which were designed to determine the extent to which status factors external to the organization (*e.g.*, social, economic and power positions in the community) are related to leadership style within the organization.

In difficult tasks involving the closely coordinated efforts of several persons, it is important that the groups be properly assembled in order to facilitate their optimum performance. The Air Force encounters this problem in manning its large bombardment aircraft. Hemphill, in his studies of crew composition, investigated the influence of leadership and other factors on effective crew performance. Hemphill has also conducted studies designed to isolate factors involved in the emergence of leadership in experimentally created groups and to test a theory in which leadership is defined as the "initiation of structure in interaction."

Shartle and Stogdill studied leadership in naval ships and shore establishments. These studies emphasized the relation of patterns of leader behavior to such factors as organization structure, interaction structures, responsibility-authority relationships, and the like.

The brief descriptions outlined above present only the central features of each series of studies. They do serve, however, to illustrate the wide scope of the program of research. The area of study ranges from a concern with factors external to the organization which condition leadership within the organization, through a concern with factors internal to the organization which have a bearing on leadership, to a concern with basic factors in group formation which are related to the emergence of leadership in its initial stages. The very scope of these studies suggests that the leadership problem is a complex one indeed.

Some of the studies have been completed. Others are still in progress. Since the Navy studies were the first to be completed, they will be most heavily represented in the present series of monographs.

The authors appreciate the support of the Office of Naval Research which financed the *Studies in Naval Leadership* under a contract (NR 171 123) with the Ohio State University Research Foundation. The authors also wish to acknowledge the valuable contributions made in all phases of the research by their colleagues on the Ohio State Leadership Studies staff.

RALPH M. STOGDILL
CARROLL L. SHARTLE

TABLE OF CONTENTS

LIST OF TABLES

LIST OF CHARTS

xv

I

INTRODUCTION

The methods described in this monograph were devised for research purposes. They were designed for use in the study of any type of organized group that has work to accomplish. The fact that the methods can be applied to the study of organizations in general represents an advantage for research purposes. It may constitute a disadvantage in situations in which specific diagnoses are required. When methods are made general enough to measure factors that are present in all organizations there exists the possibility that they may fail to measure factors that are specific to particular organizations.

The design of a research project always represents a compromise among many possible choices. The values assigned to various choices will be determined to a large extent by the objectives to be accomplished by the research.

In initiating the Ohio State Leadership Studies, it was hypothesized that the pattern of behavior exhibited in a given leadership position will be determined in part by the performance demands made upon that position. However, it was not anticipated that all the differences between leaders would be accounted for by differences in the demands made upon them by their jobs. Rather, it was hypothesized that the behavior of a leader in a given position would also be related to factors such as the following: his status in the organization hierarchy, the structure of interactions among the members of the organization, the responsibility-authority structure of the organization, and the performances of the members of the organization. In other words, leadership was viewed as one aspect of the structure and functioning of a total organization.

In accord with this formulation of the problem, it was decided to concentrate upon the task of developing methods for determining what leaders do and for measuring relevant dimensions of organization. As a result of this decision, the methods developed for the studies in naval leadership consisted of (1) interviews with administrators who were to be the subjects of the research, (2) a study of organization charts and manuals, (3) a study of the mission and objectives of the total organization and of its departments and subdivisions, (4) a modified job analysis of administrative performance, (5) a study of responsibility-authority-delegation status, (6) a sociometric study of working relationships, (7) descriptions of "leader behavior" by the leader himself and by other members of the organization, and (8) measures of individual and unit effectiveness. These methods comprise an integrated battery of research procedures.

Since it was desired to compare leaders in various types of organizations, it was necessary to devise methods which would be equally applicable in the worlds of industry, government, education, and the like. It was believed that if the general methods were designed to measure critical and essential dimensions of organization, then comparatively few of the important factors in any particular organization would be overlooked.

It was decided to collect data in quantitative rather than qualitative terms. This resulted in the development of measuring devices rather than case-study methods. The decision was based on extensive experience in the analysis of data collected by case-study methods, which were rejected for the following reasons: (1) different methods are likely to be used for the study of different types of cases; (2) data are likely to be collected on different variables for different cases; and (3) qualitative data, although collected systematically in every case, are difficult to categorize and analyze.

Since the subjects of the research were busy administrators, it was decided to reduce to a minimum the time required to fill out forms and scales. This resulted in the development of scales with lower reliabilities than is necessary for the useful prediction of individual performance. However, the leadership problem as conceived involves such a large complex of variables that it was decided to make maximum use of individual items of measurement, rather than rely upon a few highly reliable scores, each derived from a large battery of items.

Although the use of items and scales with low reliabilities requires that results be interpreted with caution for any single sample of persons or organizations, the replication of samples lends some confidence to any consistent results that may appear. Likely leads for further research may be tested later with more reliable measuring devices.

The foregoing decisions were dictated by the nature of the research task which was to be accomplished. Methods were needed which would apply to a wide variety of organizations. It was decided to study organization in terms of the behavior, status and interpersonal relationships of the members of organizations. It was decided to obtain quantitative measures of these variables for each member, rather than to observe them in a hit or miss fashion. It seemed necessary to make some sacrifice in the reliability of measurement in order to conserve the time of the subjects of the research. These decisions were made in the light of a total research design. The methods that were developed as a result of these decisions possess certain limitations which will affect their usefulness when used for purposes other than research.

This manual describes seven different methods which were employed in the study of military and business organizations. Directions for the use and administration of the forms are included in the descriptions. Data on reliability and validity are presented when these are available. The following is a list of the methods:

> The Interview
> Organization Charts and Manuals
> Sociometric Methods
> The RAD Scales
> Work Analysis Forms
> Leader Behavior Descriptions
> Effectiveness Ratings

The methods listed above constitute an integrated battery of research procedures. A number of cautions should be observed in attempting to use them for purposes other than research.

1. The methods were devised for research purposes. The data were collected in a research setting. Somewhat different results might have been obtained had the data been collected in situations where the findings were to be used for purposes of selection or evaluation.

2. The reliabilities of some of the forms are not as high as is usually desired for individual diagnosis and selection. These forms should be increased in length in order to raise their reliabilities before they are used for individual diagnosis.

3. No norms are available. The results of the research have shown that the practical significance of a given score may differ from one situation to another.

4. The methods should be regarded as tools, not as remedies. They are useful only as means of obtaining descriptions of what exists at a particular time and place. Results obtained from use of the methods cannot tell an administrator what should be done. They can serve only the purpose of providing him with information. He must then rely upon judgment in deciding what, if anything, should be done with the information.

5. The results of the research argue against the use of single measuring devices in a study of leadership. They suggest, instead, the desirability of combining organization analysis, position analysis, and personnel evaluation in an integrated set of procedures.

THE INTERVIEW

The interview employed in the leadership studies served several purposes. It provided a means for the research staff to become acquainted with the subjects and to gain an understanding of the organization. It furnished an opportunity to explain the research project and the forms to be filled out and to answer questions about them. The interview also served as a source of items for the construction of various forms and also provided a means of collecting data which were coded or assigned numerical values for purposes of classification or statistical analysis.

Data provided by the interview relative to a subject's job and unit of organization were found to be useful in setting up various analytical designs. Interview data relative to a subject's military rank, level in the organization hierarchy, length of time in his position and number of persons with whom he spent the most time on a working basis were assigned numerical scores which were treated statistically.

PURPOSE OF THE INTERVIEW FORM AND MANUAL

An interview form and a manual were prepared for the use of the staff in the field. The manual outlines the types of questions to be asked in order to elicit the information to be recorded on the interview form.

The interview was designed to elicit information from a subject relative to his duties and job, his place in the organization structure, the history and organization of his unit of organization, his problems in the management of his unit, and his working relationships with other members of the organization.

THE INTERVIEW MANUAL

The interview designed for the leadership studies is a structured, free-response type of interview. This means that the interview is designed to elicit information about specific topics, but that questions have been phrased so as to permit the interviewee to respond in his own terms.

The questions retained in the interview form are those which have proved most useful in a study of both military and business organizations. It should be recognized, however, that considerable latitude is permissable in phrasing these questions. *If the interviewee does not understand a question, it should be altered and restated, retaining its essential meaning, until it is interpreted correctly.*

Before entering into the interview proper, it is desirable to give the interviewee a brief explanation of the purpose and nature of the study in which he is asked to participate.

It has not been found necessary to request, or emphasize the necessity of, frankness in these interviews.

After introductions have been completed, explanations of the studies made, and questions answered to the satisfaction of the interviewee, it is time to enter into the interview proper.

The interviewer places the interview form on his desk in plain sight of the interviewee. He writes on this form in full view of the interviewee, and makes no attempt to conceal anything he records.

Information to Be Recorded

1. *Date*—The interviewer begins by filling in the date of the interview on the first page of the interview form.

2. *Name*—Record the full name and professional title (e.g., Capt., Dr., Rev., Prof., etc.) of the interviewee.

3. *Job Titles*—Record the official title (or titles) of the interviewee. In case the interviewee occupies more than one position, record the title of each. (For example, in naval organizations, an officer may occupy the positions of Personnel Officer, Disciplinary Officer, and Recreation Officer.)

4. *Units in Charge of*—Record the names of all the units (Departments, Divisions, Sections, etc.) headed by the interviewee. If he is not the head of any organizational unit, enter "none." The Commanding Officer or President heads the entire organization, so it is not necessary to list divisions.

5. *Units in Which a Member*—Record the names of all the units

(Departments, Divisions, Sections, etc.) in which the interviewee exercises official responsibilites, or is responsible for the performance of duties. For example, an officer may hold the position of Purchasing Officer in the Supply Department, but he may also be assigned on a part-time basis to the Records Sections of the Accounting Department.

6. *How Long Attached to This Establishment*—(Number of Months)

7. *How Long in Present Position*—(Record in Months)

8. *Past Positions Held*—(List the last three positions)

9. *Schools Attended*—(List them)

10. *Mission (objectives and functions) of Own Unit/s.*

a. *Definitions:*

The *mission* of an organization (or unit of organization) is defined in terms of its purpose and of the major general tasks it is expected to perform. The mission or general task of a given organization or unit is likely to remain more or less constant (e.g., to train personnel, to manufacture automobiles, etc.). The mission of an organization can usually be broken down into specific *objectives* which may change from time to time according to requirements of changing situations. For example, the specific objective of a training school today may be the training of a large number of cooks and bakers. Next month, it may have the specific objective of training an increased number of radio operators. The characteristic tasks of an organization (e.g., what it ordinarily does) are known as its *functions.*

Own unit may be the entire organization or a department, or division, section, etc. The following questions are designed to determine the major purpose of an organization or unit of organization.

b. *Questions:*

In a military organization, the following question will usually elicit the desired information:

"What is the mission of your (department, organization, division, section, units, etc.)?"

In a non-military organization, the following question will serve the same purpose:

"What is the primary purpose of your (department, division, section, unit or organization, etc.) ?"

If the interviewee is not in charge of any unit (department, division, etc.), but is responsible only for his individual performance, the following question may be asked:

"What are the major duties or functions of your position?"

11. *Background and History* (origin, reorganization, trend in size, major difficulties, plans for improvement) of own unit/s.

The amount of information that can be elicited relative to the history of the organization or unit will probably depend to a considerable degree upon the length of time the interviewee has been a member of the organization. It may also depend upon his position —whether or not he has access to the information. For these reasons it is not necessary to press for information on these questions, but all questions should be asked.

Questions:

a. *Origin*—"Do you know when this (establishment, station, school, company, plant, department, division, etc.) was organized? When was it started?"

b. *Reorganization*—"Has it undergone any major reorganizations since that time?"

If so, "What was the nature of the most recent of these reorganizations?"

c. *Trend in Size*—"What is the present trend in size and operations of the (organization, division, etc.)? Is it expanding, retracting or leveling off? How do you explain this trend?"

d. *Major Difficulties*—"Could you list some of the major difficulties confronting your (organization, department, etc.) at the present time?" (If the answer is "lack of money or personnel," ask if there are any others.)

e. *Plans for Solution*—"What plans do you have for solving the difficulties?"

f. *Administrative Changes*—"What administrative changes have you made in order to accommodate your personal way of doing things and in order to get the job done the way you feel it should be done?"

12. *Work of the Executive*—It is the purpose of this analysis to obtain, in an interviewee's own words, a breakdown of his work in each position he occupies. No attempt is made to have the interviewee use the items listed in the form for estimating "Time Spent in Major Responsibilities." The emphasis is on what the interviewee actually does, as he sees his own work.

Definition—A *position* is any officially designated job which is represented by an official title.

Questions:

If the interviewee occupies more than one position ask, "What per cent of time do you spend in each of your positions—what per cent in your position as .... and what per cent in your position as ....?"

If only one position is occupied ask, "What are the major duties of your position. By this I mean, how do you spend your working time? Try to think of your work on the average so as to rule out the influence of non-typical days."

The same questions can also be phrased as follows: "On the average, how do you spend your working day?" The same information should be obtained in relation to each position.

13. *Boards and Committees*—Ask the interviewee to name all of the boards and committees of which he is a member. Determine the percentage of time spent in each and the work performed in each.

14. *Organization Chart*—(for each unit supervised) showing: (a) person to whom the interviewee reports, and (b) persons who report to him.

Draw, or have the interviewee draw, an organization chart which shows his position, the position above his own, and the major positions under his direction. A chart should be drawn for each position occupied, and the relationship of these positions to each other and to higher positions in the organization should be shown.

If the interviewee has no idea of organization, the information can be obtained by asking him, "Who is your superior officer? (or) Who is the person who has authority to supervise your work? What other persons work for your superior and hold the same relation to him that you do? How many people work directly under your supervision, so that you are the one who has authority to tell them what to do? What are their names, what are their titles, what does each one of them do? Who works under each of these persons? What are their names, what do they do, etc.? How many people in all work under you?"

15. *Persons Dealt With* (in order of length of time)—It is the purpose of this section of the interview to obtain a list of those persons with whom the interviewee spends the most time on a working basis. It has been found that most persons in administrative positions spend more time with their immediate assistants and subordinates than with other persons. For this reason it appears desirable to obtain first a list, in rank order, of the assistants with whom the interviewee spends the most time. *Assistants* may include both military and civilian personnel in a military organization. *Assistants* may also include secretaries, stenographers and clerical help as well as administrative help. Unless the interviewee has only one, two or three assistants, an attempt should be made to have him name at least four or five persons.

After a list of assistants has been obtained the interviewer proceeds to obtain a list of other persons in the organization with whom the interviewee spends time on a working basis. It should be carefully emphasized and explained that this list is to include all persons in the entire organization who are not working directly under the interviewee. This includes persons who are in the same department in which he is located but who are not working under him, as well as persons in departments other than the one in which he is located.

Questions:

"I am wondering if you could list the names of your assistants with whom you spend the *most* time in getting work done. Think back over the past several weeks, consider all the persons who are working under you. With which one of these assistants have you spent the most time on a business basis? With which one have you spent the next most time? Who next? Who next? etc. What is the general kind of business you conduct with each of the persons you have named above?"

After a list of at least five or six assistants has been obtained the interviewer attempts to obtain a similar list of working partners who are not the interviewee's assistants or direct subordinates by asking the following questions of all persons except commanding officers, executive officers and presidents of companies:

Questions:

"Now, let's consider everybody in the entire (organization, school, company, etc.) who are not working under your supervision. This means that you want to consider not only the top officials but also all the members of other departments as well as the members of the (...................... department) who are not working under you. It means people who have higher level positions than yours; people at the same level as you; and those who occupy lesser positions than yours. Considering all of these people who are not your assistants, with whom do you spend the most time in getting work done? Who is next? Who is next? etc." Try to get more than five names.

After these two lists have been completed, the interviewer then requests that all of the names in the two lists be arranged in rank order by the interviewee according to the amount of time he spends with them. It may be necessary to hand the interviewee the list of names so he will have them before him. He is asked, "Consider all of the names in the two lists. With whom do you spend the most time? Rank them in order from most to least." The interviewer puts a (1) before the first, a (2) before the name of the second, and so on until all the names are ranked.

16. *Methods of Getting Best Work from Assistants*—The interviewee is asked "What do you believe are the best methods for getting your assistants to do a good job for you?"

17. *Qualifications for this Position as the Incumbent sees it.* (Training, experience and general qualifications):

The interviewee is asked, "If you were writing a set of qualifications for persons who are to fill a position similar to yours, what would you require in the way of training, experience, and other general qualifications?"

Forms to Be Filled Out By Interviewee

If there are forms to be filled out by the interviewee, present them at this time. If both interviewer and interviewee have time, the forms may be filled out while the interviewer is at hand to answer questions. If forms must be left, explain directions and mechanics of each set of forms until certain that interviewee understands clearly how to complete them. Agree upon a date and time for collecting them.

Thank the interviewee for his participation in the research. Answer any questions that he may wish to ask.

THE INTERVIEW FORM

A copy of the interview form is shown on the following pages. In the form actually used, more space was provided after each item for recording responses.

THE INTERVIEW FORM

1. Date..

2. Name..

3. Titles..

4. Units in charge of..

5. Units in which a member..
6. How long attached to this establishment?..
7. How long in present position?..
8. Previous positions held..

9. Schools attended..
10. Mission (objectives and functions) of own unit/s..

11. Background and history (origin, reorganizations, trend in size, major difficulties, plans for improvement) of own unit/s..

12. Work of the Executive: A general breakdown of work involved in each position occupied; per cent of time devoted to each position and to the administrative functions involved in each.

13. Boards and Committees and duties in each.

14. *Organization Chart* (for each unit supervised) showing: (a) person to whom responsible, and (b) persons for whom responsible.

15. Persons dealt with (in order of length of time)

<table>
<tr><td></td><td align="center">*Name or Title*
(Own Assistants (all persons directly supervised)*</td><td align="center">*Kind of Work*
Performed</td></tr>
</table>

( ) ....
( ) ....
( ) ....
( ) ....
( ) ....
( ) ....

Persons other than own assistants (all superiors, subordinates, and associates in the entire establishment, other than own assistants)*

( ) ....
( ) ....
( ) ....
( ) ....
( ) ....
( ) ....

* Determine rank order of all above, combining own assistants with persons outside own unit.

16. Methods of Getting Best Work from Assistants

17. Qualifications for this Position as the Incumbent Sees It. (Training, experience and general qualifications)

III

ORGANIZATION CHARTS AND MANUALS

A study of organization charts, organization manuals, and personnel rosters can be of considerable value in gaining an understanding of the structure of an organization. Most of the information provided by these sources can be obtained by means of interviews with top level personnel. However, the experience of the research staff indicated that even high ranking officers and executives may differ in their conceptions of the structure of an organization. When this situation was encountered, it was the practice of the research staff to request that the commanding officer or president of an organization indicate his conception of the organization by correcting the latest available edition of the organization chart to show the "present" structure of the organization. This corrected chart was accepted by the research staff as representing the "official" organization chart at the time the study was being made. When lower ranking personnel indicated conceptions of organization which deviated from the "official" organization chart, their deviations were regarded as representing perceptual error. Whatever the arguments that may be advanced in opposition to this procedure, they must be set aside, at least in military establishments, in favor of a more potent argument, namely, that the commanding officer is, with certain exceptions, empowered to assign and reassign the personnel under his command to positions (and to the duties allotted to the positions) as he may deem necessary in order to accomplish the mission of the organization. Although this power is limited by custom, by various regulations, and by the weight of what has existed and worked satisfactorily in the past, it is nevertheless true that the commanding officer may depart from the standard organization charts prescribed by higher authority when the necessity exists. In business organizations, top management is usually empowered by the corporate directors to make such changes in organization as are necessary to cope with changing conditions.

14

SCORING "LEVEL IN THE ORGANIZATION"

Organization charts were used in the leadership research to assign to each subject a score which was designated as "Level in the Organization." This is an arbitrary score which assigns equal numerical values to all the positions in the same echelon of organization. It represents a measure of vertical differentiation. Chart I illustrates the method of assigning such scores.

Organizations which are structured entirely on a line basis present little difficulty in assigning scores for "level." However, problems are encountered in organizations which contain both line and staff positions. Results of the research suggest that the president and vice president (or commanding officer and executive officer) should be assigned different scores. Aides, staff assistants and *assistants to* unit heads should be assigned a level score which is at least one step below the echelon of their immediate superiors. However, *assistant unit heads,* who act with the full authority of their unit heads, should be assigned the same level score as that assigned to their immediate superiors. This system of scoring combines on the same level those persons who exhibit more nearly similar patterns of performance.

It may be seen in Chart I, that the president has been assigned a score of 9; the vice president, a score of 8; the division heads, a score of 7; the department heads, a score of 6; and so on down the line. The administrative assistant to the vice president receives a score of 7, as does the assistant division head in Division A. The assistant to Department Head B₂ receives a score of 5. Branch Head 22 and his line assistant also receive scores of 5. This method of scoring assigns higher scores to higher level positions, and also differentiates between line and staff positions.

A maximum score of nine was decided upon as a convenience in IBM computation. Due to the fact that some organizations are more steeply stratified than others, it is necessary to begin numbering with the top position, rather than with the bottom positions, in order for the scores to have the same value and meaning from one organization to another.

CHART 1. Scores for Level in Organization

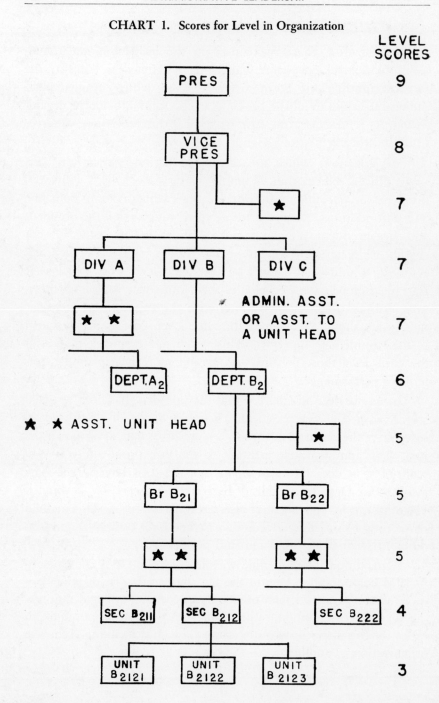

OTHER USES OF CHARTS AND MANUALS

Organization charts have served another important function in the research. Sociometric diagrams have been superimposed on organization charts in order to compare the structure of working relationships among the members with the formal organization structure.

Organization manuals which outline the duties of the various positions within an organization are of value in gaining an understanding of the formally defined responsibilities of the persons (or positions) being studied.

Personnel rosters, used in conjunction with organization charts, are of value in selecting samples of subjects in the event that it is impossible to study all members of an organization.

Other records that were employed in the leadership studies include operational readiness reports, inspection board reports, re-enlistment records, personnel turnover records, disciplinary records of enlisted personnel, financial reports, production records, and the like. Such records are of value as sources of data which can be used as measures of organization effectiveness.

IV

SOCIOMETRIC METHODS

Sociometry is a method which was devised for measuring the structure of preference relationships existing among the members of a social group. In military and industrial use this method is known as the "nominating technique" or the "buddy-rating technique."

The basic method requires each member of a group to express a preference as to which members of his group he would most want for leader or roommate, or the like. Using such expressions of choice, a sociogram can be constructed showing how many times each member is chosen and by whom he is chosen. Chart 2 represents such a sociogram. The sociogram shows that person B is

CHART 2. Sociogram of an Informal Group

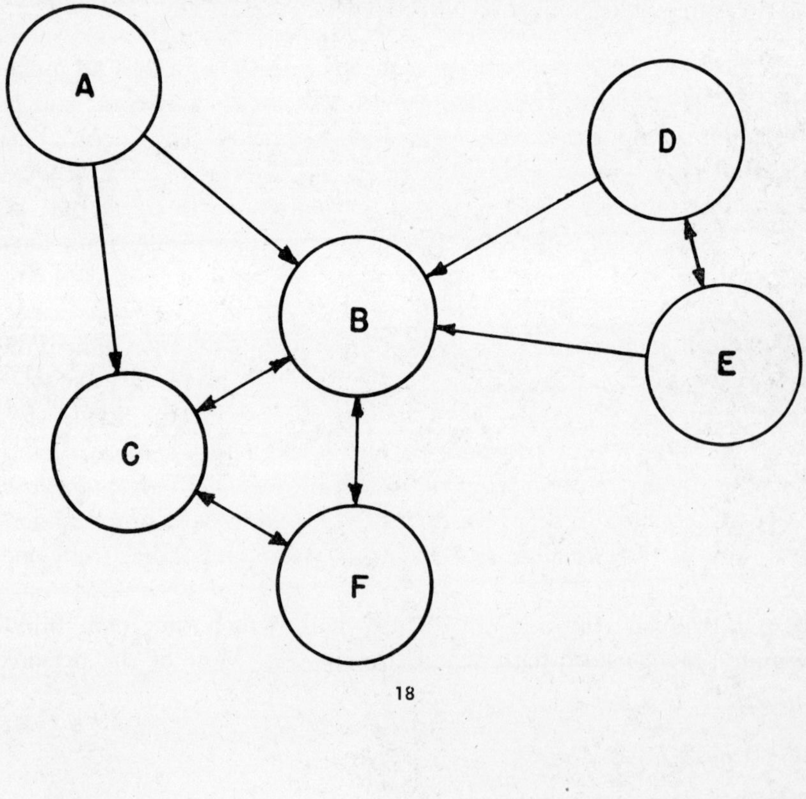

chosen by all members of the group. B, C, and F choose each other, D and E are each chosen once, but A receives no choices. F receives two, and C receives three choices.

THE SOCIOMETRIC QUESTIONS

The basic question utilized for obtaining the data relative to the actual work associations of respondents was stated as follows: *"With whom do you spend the most time in getting work done?"* It was found necessary as the studies progressed to add clarifying instructions in such a manner as to eliminate the influence of atypical days. An officer might reply, for example, "Well yesterday I spent most of my time with an officer who has just reported for duty." In order to overcome this type of difficulty the following instructions were added to the original question: *"Think back over the past month. Consider all members of the organization here that you have contacted during business hours. With which ones have you spent the most time on a business basis? With whom, on the average, do you spend the most time in getting work done?"* (See item 15 in *The Interview Form,* Section II.)

Each person interviewed was encouraged to name several members, to describe the kinds of business transacted with each, and to rank the names in order according to amount of time spent. This method was later modified in order to overcome an additional difficulty. It was found that some officers tended to think only of their assistants and subordinates, while others tended to think only of superiors and associates at the same level in other departments. In the revised procedure, the person being interviewed was asked to name first, his assistants and subordinates in his own unit with whom he spent the most time, and, second, to name the superiors and persons at the same and in lower echelons in other units. He was then asked to consider the names in both lists combined, and to rank them in order according to time spent. This procedure appears necessary in order for each person to have a common understanding of the problem, and to obtain data comparable from one person to another.

Individuals differ in the facility with which they can differentiate among those with whom they work. Most of the persons interviewed were able to name the first two or three persons with a high degree of confidence. Some could name seven or eight work partners and express complete satisfaction with the order in which they were ranked. A fairly large number ranked the fourth, fifth, and succeeding persons with a diminishing degree of certainty. A very few stated that they were unable to discriminate among their immediate juniors, maintaining that they spent about an equal amount of time with each of them. Analysis of logs of working contacts in one organization indicated that this was a correct statement of the situation for some persons.

It will be noted that the above description of method is based on questions relating to actual, not preferred, associations with other persons. To ask a member to name those with whom he *actually spends time* is not equivalent to asking him to name those with whom he would *prefer to spend his time:* The latter, a statement of preference, might be used as a criterion of leadership popularity. However, time actually spent with other persons in a formally structured organization may be determined not by personal choice, but by working proximity, lines of communication, work routing, requirements for coordination, emergency demands, and the like. Working sociometry, based on time spent with other persons, would appear to represent a measure of operative organization, rather than leadership preference. The structure of working relationships and the structure of leadership preferences are significantly correlated, but are by no means identical, as is pointed out in the discussion of Table 5.

THE SOCIOGRAM AND THE ORGANIZATION CHART

The list of names obtained by means of the sociometric questions (item 15 of the interview, in Section II) can be used to construct a sociogram which is superimposed on the organization chart. Such a sociogram provides a picture of the structure of working interrelationships among the members of an organization.

Chart 3 illustrates a sociogram superimposed on an organization chart. It will be observed that the Commanding Officer (CO) mentions the Executive Officer (XO) and Department Head C as the two persons with whom he spends the most time in working contacts. The Commanding Officer is mentioned by the Executive

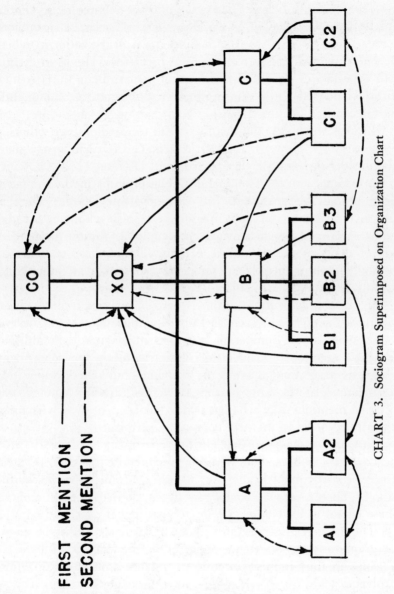

FIRST MENTION ——————
SECOND MENTION — — — —

CHART 3. Sociogram Superimposed on Organization Chart

Officer, Department Head C and Division Head C1 as one of the two persons with whom they spend the most time on a working basis. Only the first two persons mentioned by each member are shown here in order that the chart will not be too complicated.

The Executive Officer (XO) mentions the Commanding Officer and Department Head B as work partners. The Executive Officer is mentioned by six persons. In most naval organizations studied the Executive Officer receives the most mentions. This is in accord with expectation, since it is his function to coordinate the activities of the organization and to insure that the policies of the Commanding Officer are put into effect.

In Department A, the members tend to mention each other as work partners. However, in Department C, the members tend to mention persons outside the department. Division Head C1 tends to work more with the Commanding Officer and with Department Head B than he does with his own department head. Such a pattern of working relationships is likely to be exhibited by the Public Information Officer when he occupies a position lower than that of department head. The Commanding Officer is likely to consult with him directly on public relations matters rather than dealing with the department head.

In most organizations studied there have been found one or two department heads, such as Department Head B, who receive an unusually large number of mentions. Interview data indicate that these mentions are likely to concentrate upon the department head who is at the focus of the activities and objectives of the organizations at the time of the study. As activities change, the focus of mentions may change to the department which is most critically involved in the new tasks to be performed.

In Chart 3, it is seen that all the department heads work with the Executive Officer. The division heads tend to work with their respective department heads, thus insuring intradepartment coordination. There are two contacts between departments B and C. These lateral contacts facilitate interdepartmental coordination.

The method illustrated in Chart 3 has practical utility in showing graphically those areas of organization in which working relationships are most highly concentrated, and the units of organization involved.

THE NUMBER OF MENTIONS TO BE CHARTED

There are no set rules for determining how many mentions per individual should be plotted. However, it should be pointed out that if each person in an organization of five members is given four mentions, then each member will receive four mentions, and the scores will have no discriminating value. No matter how many mentions are finally used, there is much insight to be gained by plotting the first two mentions and making a count of scores and an inspection of the chart to see which members receive the most first and second mentions. The third mention may then be added to the chart, and then succeeding mentions.

In a naval shore station in which 44 officers were interviewed, the total number of mentions received (MR score) based upon the first three mentions is correlated .91 with the MR score based on the first four mentions. However, the MR score based on three mentions is correlated only .83 with the MR score based on all mentions. The correlation of MR based on four mentions is correlated .94 with MR scores based on all mentions. As a rule of thumb, it would seem desirable to plot at least four mentions when the number of members of an organization exceeds twenty. The correlation of .94 between MR (four mentions) and MR (all mentions) suggests that not much information is lost if only the first four mentions are plotted for each member of an organization of 40 persons. It is also apparent that the scores become meaningless if each person is given approximately as many mentions as there are members of the organization.

TWENTY SOCIOMETRIC INDICES

In order to move from a pictorial to a quantitative level of description, several indices were derived from the MG (mentions-given) and MR (mentions-received) scores. These indices are listed and defined in Table I. One may mention other members within one's own unit of organization (GI), or one may mention others outside one's own unit (GO). One may mention seniors (GA), peers (GS), and juniors (GB). One may receive mentions from members within (RI) and outside (RO) one's own unit and from seniors (RA), peers (RS), and juniors (RB).

Other indices besides those listed in Table 1 were derived, but they have proved to be rather insubstantial in that they result mostly in zero scores. Two of the indices (G$_2$B and R$_2$A) listed in Table 1,

TABLE 1—Definitions of Twenty Sociometric Indices

Sociometric Indices	Definitions of Indices
Mentions Given	
MG	Total number of persons mentioned
GI	*Inside* own unit of organization
GO	*Outside* own unit of organization (persons in other units are named)
GA	To persons in echelons *above* one's own
GS	To persons in the *same* echelon as one's own
GB	To persons in echelons *below* one's own
G_2A	To persons in echelons 2 *or more levels above* one's own
G_2B	To persons in echelons 2 *or more levels below* one's own
NEG	Number of echelons into which mentions are given
Mentions Received	
MR	Total number of mentions received
RI	*Inside* one's own unit of organization
RO	From persons in units *other* than one's own
RA	From persons in echelons *above* own
RS	From persons in *same* echelon
RB	From persons *below* own
R_2B	From echelons 2 *or more levels below* own
R_2A	From echelons 2 *or more levels above* own
NER	Number of echelons from which mentions are received
RM	Number of reciprocated mentions
MR/P	Number of mentions received divided by number of members within own unit minus self

are examples of such insubstantial scores. This fact may be observed in Table 2, which illustrates a convenient method for plotting and counting scores for the various indices.

In the left hand column of Table 2 are listed the persons who give mentions to other members of the organization. In the top row are listed the members who receive mentions from those listed at the left. It will be observed that the CO gives mentions to XO, A, B, and B₃. Moving to the right hand section of the table, his total of four mentions given is recorded under MG. His mention given to the XO is entered under GI. He has no superiors or peers in the organization so zero scores are entered under GA, GS, and G₂A. His four mentions are given to juniors and are entered under GB. Three mentions are given to members who are removed two or more echelons below his own (G₂B). He gives mentions to persons in three separate vertical echelons (NEG). He gives three mentions (to XO, B, and B₃) which are reciprocated (RM).

The count of mentions-received scores moves down from the

TABLE 2—Count of Sociometric Scores

Receivers*

Givers*	CO	XO	A	A₁	A₂	B	B₁	B₂	B₃	C	C₁	Total
CO		*1*	*3*			*2*						
XO	*4*		*2*			*1*				*3*		
A		*1*	*3*		*4*	*2*				*3*		
A₁	*1*	*2*	*3*									
A₂	*1*	*2*	*3*									
B	*2*	*1*	*3*				*3*	*3*	*4*			
B₁						*1*		*3*				
B₂		*2*				*1*	*3*					
B₃	*3*	*2*				*1*						
C	*2*	*1*	*3*			*4*						
C₁	·									*1*		
												Total
MR	6	9	6	0	1	8	1	1	2	3	0	37
RI	1	1	2	0	1	3	1	1	1	1	0	12
RO	5	8	4	0	0	5	0	0	1	2	0	25
RA	0	1	2	0	0	2	0	0	2	1	0	8
RS	0	0	2	0	1	2	1	1	0	1	0	8
RB	6	8	2	0	0	4	0	0	0	1	0	21
R₂B	5	5	0	0	0	0	0	0	0	0	0	10
R₂A	0	0	1	0	0	1	0	0	1	0	0	3
NER	3	3	4	0	1	4	1	1	2	3	0	22
MR/P	1/1	1/1	6/2	0/2	1/2	8/3	1/3	1/3	2/3	3/1	0/1	

Mentions Received

Mentions Given

	MG	GI	GO	GA	GS	GB	G₂A	G₂B	NEG	RM
CO	4	1	3	0	0	4	0	3	3	3
XO	4	1	3	1	0	3	0	0	2	4
A	3	0	3	1	2	0	0	0	2	3
A₁	4	2	2	3	1	0	2	0	4	0
A₂	4	1	3	4	0	0	2	0	3	0
B	4	1	3	2	1	1	1	0	4	4
B₁	3	2	1	2	1	0	1	0	3	1
B₂	3	2	1	2	1	0	1	0	3	1
B₃	3	1	2	3	0	0	2	0	3	2
C	4	0	4	2	2	0	1	0	3	2
C₁	1	1	0	1	0	0	0	0	1	0
	37	12	25	21	8	8	10	3	31	20

* Italicized figures indicate persons mentioned 1st, 2nd, 3rd and 4th.

Checks

MG = GI + GO
MG = GA + GS + GB
MR = RI + RO
MR = RA + RS + RB

MG = MR
GI = RI
GO = RO
GB = RA
GS = RS
GA = RB

top of the table. Department Head A receives six mentions, which are recorded after (MR) in the lower left segment of the chart. He receives two mentions from members (A_1, A_2) within his own unit (RI). He receives four mentions from persons outside his unit (RO). He receives two mentions from seniors (RA), two from peers (RS), and two from juniors (RB). He receives no mentions from members two or more echelons below his own (R_2B), and only one from a member (the CO) who is two or more echelons above his own (R_2A). He receives mentions from members who are located in four different echelons of the organization (NER). His total mention-received score (MR) is six. There are only two members besides himself in his unit of organization. Therefore his MR/P score is 6/2 or 3.0.

Scores such as those described above serve to indicate whether a member tends to work with members within his own unit or with members outside his unit, and whether he tends to work with seniors, peers, or juniors.

RELIABILITY OF THE SOCIOMETRIC INDICES

In order to test the reliability of the indices described above, a naval district command staff was studied twice. Thirty-four officers were interviewed. The same staff was restudied a month later. Thirty-two officers participated in both studies.

The means, standard deviations and correlation coefficients derived from data provided by officers who participated in both the first and second studies are shown in Table 3. All mentions given by each officer were used in computing the scores.

It will be noted that more persons, on the average, were mentioned during the restudy than during the first study. It is possible, and probable, that this difference is less an expression of organization change than of a greater feeling of confidence on the part of the officers being interviewed in the motives and purposes of the interviewers in obtaining such data.

The correlation coefficients in the right hand column range from .10 for GS to .97 for RB. The test-retest correlations of mentions-given scores (MG, GI, GO, GA, GS, GB, G_2A and NEG) range from .10 to .82. The mentions-received scores (MR, RI, RO, RA, RS, RB, R_2B, NER and MR/P) are considerably higher. These

TABLE 3—Test-Retest Correlations of Eighteen Sociometric Variables:
Means and Standard Deviations

(N = 32 Commissioned Officers)

Sociometric Indices	First Study		Second Study		
	M	SD	M	SD	r
Mentions Given					
MG	2.8	1.5	3.7	1.9	.57
GI	1.6	1.2	2.2	1.6	.73
GO	1.2	1.3	1.5	1.2	.60
GA	1.5	1.0	2.0	1.3	.79
GS	.4	1.1	.8	.7	.10
GB	.8	1.3	.9	1.1	.74
G_2A	.6	1.2	1.0	.8	.82
NEG	2.2	1.0	2.8	1.1	.64
Mentions Received					
MR	2.8	2.9	3.7	2.8	.92
RI	1.6	2.2	2.2	2.2	.89
RO	1.2	2.2	1.5	2.4	.85
RA	.8	1.2	.9	1.2	.72
RS	.4	.9	.8	1.0	.57
RB	1.5	2.5	2.0	2.5	.97
R_2B	.6	1.8	1.0	2.3	.93
NER	1.5	1.7	2.2	1.4	.76
RM	1.0	1.1	1.9	1.7	.78
MR/P	1.0	1.1	1.8	1.2	.79

r = .45 is significant at the .05 level.
r = .35 is significant at the .01 level.

range from .57 to .97. The correlations for MR, RB, and R₂B are above .90. If these test-retest correlations are regarded as reliability coefficients it is apparent that the mentions-received scores are more reliable than the mentions-given scores for this organization.

It should be pointed out that MG is a function of the individual, while MR is a function of the group in relation to the individual. The group scores appear to be considerably more stable than the individual scores.

VALIDITY OF THE INDICES

Data derived from the study of a naval air station permit an approximate determination of validity of the sociometric scores. In the course of interviewing 44 commissioned officers, each was asked to name the other officers on the station with whom he spent the most time in getting work done.

During the second week in which interviews were being conducted, the officers were asked to keep a log of work performance. The log sheet was marked off in one minute intervals from 8:00 A.M. to 5:00 P.M., so that the end of one kind of work performance or personal contact and the beginning of another kind of performance or contact with another person could be indicated by a check mark at the appropriate hour and minute of the day. Kinds of work performance were coded so that kind of work being done could be indicated on the log by a code number. Similarly the names of persons contacted were indicated on the log by code letters.

Examination of the logs indicated that the 32 officers who kept the log during the three-day period contacted an average of 14 persons each daily. Six of these persons were other officers within the organization. Eight of the persons contacted were enlisted or civilian personnel or persons outside the organization. Only time spent in making contacts with other commissioned officers within the organization was used in computing the logged sociometric score. Time spent in formal staff conferences was not included because few officers listed the names of all persons attending the staff meetings.

Most of the logs showed multiple contacts with certain persons during the day. The total daily time spent with single individuals ranged from 1 to 150 minutes. Approximately half the persons contacted involved less than ten minutes of working time daily.

Each officer's logged sociometric scores consisted of the total time logged over a three-day period with each person whom he contacted. In general, unless an officer spent more than 20 minutes in working time with another officer during the three-day period, that contact was omitted from the sociometric chart. This cutting point was adopted on the assumption that working interactions of longer total duration might be more representative (i.e. less subject to determination by chance circumstances) than shorter contacts. Although the average officer contacted 14 persons daily, only 6 of these contacts were with other officers in the organization, and some of these were of too short duration to show on the sociometric charts. It is for this reason that the average number of mentions given and received is lower for the logged time than for the estimated time (Table 4).

It was possible to determine for each officer the amount of time logged as having been spent with other officers during the three-day period. These logged time scores can be used to construct sociograms and derive sociometric indices in the same manner that mentions are used. Since logged time represents a comparatively accurate measure of time spent with other persons, it might be used as a criterion score.

TABLE 4—Correlation of Logged Time with Estimated Time for Eighteen Sociometric Indices: Means and Standard Deviations

(N = 32 Commissioned Officers)

Sociometric Indices	Log (Criterion)		Estimate		
	M	SD	M	SD	r
Mentions Given					
MG	3.3	1.4	4.2	2.0	.45
GI	1.8	1.1	2.1	1.6	.58
GO	1.5	1.3	2.1	1.6	.53
GA	1.4	1.3	2.0	1.6	.47
GS	1.0	.9	1.4	1.1	.20
GB	.9	1.3	.8	1.3	.84
G_2A	.5	.8	.7	1.1	.85
NEG	2.4	.9	2.4	.8	.46
Mentions Received					
MR	3.3	2.4	4.2	2.9	.65
RI	1.8	1.7	2.1	1.8	.73
RO	1.5	1.6	2.1	2.8	.65
RA	.9	1.3	.8	1.1	.69
RS	1.0	1.1	1.4	1.3	.36
RB	1.4	2.1	2.0	2.6	.71
R_2B	.5	1.3	.7	1.8	.82
NER	2.0	1.0	2.0	1.0	.52
RM	1.6	1.2	1.9	1.7	.59
MR/P	2.2	1.3	2.4	1.5	.46

r = .45 is significant at the .05 level.
r = .35 is significant at the .01 level.

The correlations between estimated time and logged time are shown in Table 4. Among the mentions-given scores, time logged as spent with juniors (GB) and with persons two or more echelons above own (G_2A) are most highly correlated with estimated time with these persons. The correlation of .20 for GS indicates that estimates and the log are not in close agreement as to time spent with peers.

Among the mentions-received scores, the number of mentions

received from persons two or more echelons below one's own (R_2B) are most highly correlated with the logged scores. The correlation is .82. All the mentions-received scores are significantly correlated with their respective criterion or log scores. All except RS, and NER are correlated above .60 with the criterion scores. In the field of personnel studies, tests with this level of validity are generally regarded as useful for selection purposes. Number of mentions received from juniors (RB) is correlated .71 with the corresponding score obtained from the log, while the correlation between logged scores and estimated scores is .73 for mentions received within own unit (RI).

If log scores may be accepted as criteria, then the most valid measures of working relationships for the sample under study are GB, R_2B and G_2A. However, GI, MR, RI, RO, RA, RB, and RM are also highly enough correlated with their respective criteria to be regarded as valid measures of working relationships.

RELATION OF SOCIOMETRIC INDICES TO OTHER MEASURES

The correlation of the sociometric indices with several other measures is shown in Table 5. It will be observed that GI, GA, NEG, G_2A and RA are negatively correlated with level. This is in accord with expectation, since those in the highest echelons have few seniors to whom they can give mentions and those in the lowest echelon can mention only seniors or peers. GB is positively correlated to a fairly high degree with level. MR, RO, RB, R_2B, NER, RM and MR/P are also positively and significantly correlated with level. Those in the higher echelons tend to be mentioned more frequently as work partners. These results suggest that some types of working relationships in operative organization are probably conditioned to a fairly high degree by the general formal structure of a naval organization.

It may also be seen that those officers who give mentions to persons outside their units (GO), to seniors (GA) and to peers (GS) tend to receive fewer nominations for "best leader" from enlisted men. Those who are mentioned most frequently by persons within their own units (RI) tend to receive a significantly large number of nominations for "best leader."

Those officers who receive more total mentions (MR), more mentions from juniors (RB) and fewer mentions from outsiders (RO) are rated higher in military leadership by their senior officers. Those who give more mentions to outsiders, seniors and peers (GO, GA and GS), and who receive more mentions from those persons (RO, RA, and RS) are described by juniors as engaging

TABLE 5—Correlation of Sociometric Indices with Level, Best-Leader Nominations, Military Leadership and Integration

Sociometric Indices[a]	Level[b]	"Best Leader"[c] Nominations	Military[c] Leadership	Integration[c]
Mentions Given		Correlation Coefficients		
MG	.04	..	..	..
GI	—.25	.14	.03	.04
GO	.38[d]	—.23	.10	—.29[d]
GA	—.50[e]	—.31[d]	—.04	—.34[d]
GS	.07	—.24	.02	—.35[a]
GB	.64[e]	.18	.15	.10
G_2A	—.53[e]	..	..	..
NEG	—.01	..	..	..
Mentions Received				
MR	.59[e]	.23	.28[d]	.26[d]
RI	.21	.35[e]	.06	.51[e]
RO	.69[e]	—.08	—.36[e]	—.27[d]
RA	—.29	.00	.03	—.18
RS	.09	—.14	.11	—.23
RB	.82[e]	.23	.26[d]	.29[d]
R_2B	.79[e]	..	..	..
NER	.60[e]	..	..	..
RM	.46[e]	..	..	..
MR/P	.77[e]	..	..	..

[a] See Table I for definitions of indices.
[b] N = 42 officers on a cruiser.
[c] N = 62 officers on submarines.
[d] Significant at .05 level.
[e] Significant at .01 level.

less frequently in integrating behavior. Those officers who receive more total mentions (MR), mentions from persons in own unit (RI), and from juniors (RB) are described by enlisted men as engaging more frequently in integrative behavior. The correlations between sociometric scores and other leader-behavior scales (organization, communication, representation, and relations with juniors) follow a similar pattern.

USE OF WORK SOCIOMETRY

It has been shown that the sociometric indices are not highly correlated with such criteria of leadership quality as ratings by seniors and nominations by juniors. Preference sociometry appears to be more useful than work sociometry for establishing leadership criteria.

Sociometric methods herein described would appear to be most useful for determining the relationship between formal structure and the structure of working relationships in an organization. This relationship may be shown by superimposing a sociogram on the formal organization chart, or by correlating the sociometric indices with other measures.

V

RESPONSIBILITY, AUTHORITY AND
DELEGATION SCALES
(THE RAD SCALES)

DEVELOPMENT AND USE OF THE RAD SCALES

The RAD Scales were designed to measure different degrees of perceived responsibility, authority and delegation as exhibited by individuals who occupy administrative or supervisory positions. They may be used by an individual for purposes of indicating the nature of his own perceived responsibility, authority and delegation, or they may be used by an observer to describe another person. An attempt has been made to state the items in such general terms that they may be applied in any formally structured organization.

Scale Construction

The first step in constructing the RAD Scales was to collect a large number of items describing different degrees or levels of responsibility, a second set of items describing authority, and a third set describing delegation. The items were collected from staff members of the Personnel Research Board and from graduate students in classes in Industrial Psychology. A large percentage of the students had served in the armed forces as commissioned officers, and a considerable percentage had been employed in a variety of industrial and business concerns.

The three sets of items were edited and prepared in mimeographed form in such a manner that each item could be given a numerical value ranging from zero through eight. The scaling method is essentially a modification of Thurstone's method of equal appearing intervals.[1]

The same students who constructed lists of items also "sorted" them for purposes of obtaining scale values. However, instead of sorting the items into numbered piles, the sorters were instructed

[1] Thurstone, L. L., and Chave, E. J. *The Measurement of Attitude* (Chicago: University of Chicago Press, 1929).

to indicate the scale value of each item on a mimeographed list. The directions for sorting items for the Responsibility Scale were as follows:

> Please sort (or rate) the following items on a scale of (0) to (8) to indicate the degree of responsibility represented by the item.
>
> Let (8) represent the highest possible degree of responsibility.
>
> Let (7) (6) (5) represent decreasing degrees.
>
> Let (4) represent a neutral (neither high nor low) degree.
>
> Let (3) (2) (1) represent decreasing degrees.
>
> Let (0) represent the lowest possible degree of responsibility.

TABLE 6—Mean Scale Values of Items in Scales I to VI
(Based on Scale ranging from 0 through 8)

Item Number[a]	Scale I Responsibility	Scale II Authority	Scale III Delegation	Scale IV Responsibility	Scale V Authority	Scale VI Delegation
1	7.3	7.7	7.8	7.4	7.9	7.2
2	6.5	7.0	6.6	6.4	7.0	6.5
3	5.0	5.6	5.8	5.0	5.7	5.7
4	3.9	5.0	4.6	4.0	5.0	4.6
5	3.0	3.7	3.6	3.1	3.8	3.6
6	2.3	3.0	2.7	1.8	3.3	2.3
7	1.4	2.2	1.2	1.0	2.5	1.6
8	0.5	1.0	.7	0.0	1.3	.3

[a] See the various RAD Scales for the list of items composing each scale.

The average scale values of the items are shown in Table 6. Since items with wide dispersion values were rejected, the use of means rather than median scale values does not give undue weight to the results of sorters who deviated one or two scale steps from their fellow sorters in assigning scale values to an item.

A variety of formats and scoring methods was tried on an experimental basis. The scales were revised after each study of an organization. New items were constructed on three separate occasions. On the third revision more than 2,600 items were collected. From these the 90 most promising items for each scale were selected for temporary use on the basis of range of scale values and small standard deviations of scale values, as determined by the sorting of 47 graduate students. In each item analysis those items were retained which contributed most toward interval consistency (correlation of item with total score of two scales combined), and reliability (correlation of two different forms of the same scale).

Results with the first experimental scales indicated that the scores were non-differentiating when subjects were requested to check all items descriptive of their own situations. Poor *scale vs. scale* reliabilities were obtained when subjects checked only the single most descriptive item in each scale. Highest reliabilities were obtained when the two most descriptive items in each scale were checked, and when a Likert type of scaling[2] was employed. In Table 7 the reliability coefficients obtained by three methods of

TABLE 7—Reliability Coefficients Under Three Methods of Scoring
(*Scale Versus Scale Correlations*)

Scale	Thurstone Scale		Likert Scale
	Single Best Item	Average of Two Items	Total— All Items
R (Responsibility)	.17	.42	.46
A (Authority)	.27	.40	.44
D (Delegation)	.21	.30	.44

scoring are shown. The subjects were 18 commissioned officers in advanced graduate training. Each officer described his last military billet before enrolling in the university. Although a Likert scale yields slightly higher reliabilities, it was decided to use a Thurstone-type scale because of its ease of administration and scoring. Also, as may be seen in Table 7, a Thurstone score based on the average of 2 items from each scale yielded reliabilities almost as high as those obtained by the Likert scoring.

In a Thurstone-type scale one arbitrarily selected extreme of the scale is assumed to represent a zero point on a continuum. For the RAD Scales, it cannot be assumed that the zero points of any two scales, even though they measure the same continuum (e.g., responsibility), occupy the same point on a continuum represented by a universe of such scales. For this reason, a score of 6.5 on one scale cannot be regarded as necessarily equivalent to a score of 6.5 on another scale.

[2] Likert, R. A Technique for the Measurement of Attitudes. *Archives of Psychology*, No. 140, 1932.

The scaling method merely served as a means for ordering the items on a continuum so that they are separated by somewhat less than one full scale step, on the average. In order to avoid the appearance of a degree of accuracy and refinement which is not present in the scales, the computed scale values of the items were replaced by numbers ranging from 1 to 8. The correlation between scores obtained with the substitute scale values and scores obtained with the computed scale values is .99+ for two different samples.

Reliability

The RAD Scales were subjected to nine different revisions, primarily with the aim of improving reliability. The maximum

TABLE 8—Reliability Coefficients of RAD Scales

Type of Organization	Number of Subjects	Reliability Coefficients		
		Responsibility	Authority	Delegation
		Scale I vs. IV	Scale II vs. V	Scale III vs. VI
Air Station	39	.83	.72	.73
Submarines	69	.60	.57	.83
Command Staff	22	.70	.75	.79
LSTs (I)[a]	48	.66	.72	.39
LSTs (II)[a]	46	.80	.28	.86
District Staff (I)[b]	34	.73	.82	.60
District Staff (II)[b]	33	.70	.68	.90
School Principals	73	.88	.81	.78

[a] The landing ships (LST) were studied twice, with approximately six months intervening.
[b] The district comamnd staff was studied twice, with approximately one month intervening.

possible range of scores in the final forms was from 1.5 to 7.5. Since subjects tend to check items with the higher scale values, the range of scores is further reduced. When scores are so markedly attenuated, it is difficult to obtain high reliability coefficients. In Table 8 are shown the reliability coefficients (corrected by the Spearman-Brown formula) when the average of two items checked in Scale I (Responsibility) is correlated with the average of two items checked in Scale IV (Responsibility), when Scale II (Authority) is correlated with Scale V (Authority), and when Scale III (Delegation) is correlated with Scale VI (Delegation).

Another source of evidence relative to the reliabilities of the scales is provided by those organizations which were studied on two separate occasions. A naval district command staff was studied twice, with one month intervening. The test-retest correlations of the RAD Scales for 32 officers who filled out the forms on both occasions are .62 for Responsibility and .55 for Authority. The test-retest correlation for Delegation is .73. These should be regarded as minimum reliabilities, since it is probable that the correlations were lowered by changes in the organization. The addition to the staff of a high echelon officer as a department head during the interval between the two studies probably changed the responsibility and authority status of a number of officers.

Validity

No claims are made for the validity of the RAD Scales. Responses to the scales represent merely what a subject is willing to

TABLE 9—Correlation Between Self-Descriptions and Descriptions by Subordinates and Superiors on the RAD Scales

Type of Organization	Persons Described	Number Described	Correlations		
			R	A	D
Air Station	Subordinates[a]	41	.71	.22	.39
Research Staff	Superiors[b]	47	.65	.33	.28

[a] In the Naval Air Station, the same superior in some instances described several subordinates.

[b] In a Naval Air Research and Development Command, the score of each superior was correlated with the average score of two subordinates who described his behavior.

say about his responsibility, authority and delegation. An observer's perception of a subject's responsibility, authority and delegation can hardly be regarded as an adequate criterion, because it is highly probable that an observer's perception of his own responsibility and authority may condition his perceptions of another's responsibility and authority.

There is a tendency for persons in administrative positions to perceive their own responsibility (or authority) as it is perceived by their subordinates and superiors. The data shown in Table 9 reveal a positive correlation between self-descriptions and descriptions by others. These results also indicate much greater agreement between self-reports and reports by subordinates and superiors in describing responsibility than in describing authority or delegation.

Administration and Scoring

The RAD Scales are self-administering. They may be administered individually or in groups. The instructions require the subject to double check (✓✓) the most descriptive item in each scale and to check (✓) the next most descriptive item. Since there are two scales that measure responsibility, for example, the score for R is obtained by computing the sum of the four items checked in the two scales and dividing the sum by four.

The scoring key is the same for each of the six scales. The item scores for each scale are shown below. A high score indicates a high degree of estimated responsibility, authority or delegation.

Scoring Key

Item Number	Scale Value
1	8
2	7
3	6
4	5
5	4
6	3
7	2
8	1

The score for R (Responsibility) is the sum of the four items checked in Scales I and IV divided by four.

$$R = \frac{\text{Scale I (2 items)} + \text{Scale IV (2 items)}}{4}$$

The score for A (Authority) is the sum of the four items checked in Scales II and V divided by four.

$$A = \frac{\text{Scale II (2 items)} + \text{Scale V (2 items)}}{4}$$

The score for D (Delegation) is the sum of the four items checked in Scales III and VI divided by four.

$$D = \frac{\text{Scale III (2 items)} + \text{Scale VI (2 items)}}{4}$$

Because of the simplicity of the scoring method, no separate scoring key is provided.

Norms

There are no norms for the RAD Scales. The use of norms in personnel testing implies the establishment of reference points against which practical considerations may be weighed. It will be necessary to accumulate a large body of information before any idea can be gained regarding what is a "normal" degree of responsibility or authority for a particular type of administrative position in any given type of organization.

TABLE 10—Average R, A and D Scores of Commissioned Officers in Various Navy Positions

Type of Position	Type of Organization	N	Average Score[a]		
			R	A	D
Accounting Officer	Command Staff	4	7.3	6.5	5.2
Administrative Ass't.	Shore Station	6	5.4	5.2	5.2
Chief of Staff	Command Staff	4	7.0	6.5	5.3
Commander	Command Staff	6	5.8	5.6	7.2
Commanding Officer	Submarines	9	6.7	7.4	7.0
Commanding Officer	Destroyers	3	6.5	7.0	7.0
Education Officer	Bureau	5	5.0	5.2	5.5
Engineering Officer	Submarines	10	6.2	5.7	5.6
Engineering Officer	LSTs	9	4.9	5.1	5.7
Executive Officer	Submarines	10	5.7	5.6	6.4
Executive Officer	Destroyers	3	6.0	6.0	6.0
Legal Officer	Shore Station	4	6.3	6.3	4.3
Operations Officer	Command Staff	6	6.7	5.0	6.1
Operations Officer	Submarines	5	4.6	4.8	3.6
Personnel Officer	Bureau	6	5.5	5.5	6.7
Personnel Officer	Command Staff	4	5.0	4.3	4.3
Public Information	C. N. O.	8	6.0	5.3	4.7
Supply Officer	Command Staff	6	7.0	6.5	6.0
Supply Officer	Submarines	7	5.6	5.3	5.9
Training Officer	Bureau	7	7.1	5.9	6.9
Training Officer	Shore Station	5	7.0	4.6	5.8

[a] Based on rating scales with values ranging from a low of 1 through a high of 8.

The data in the table above are presented, not as norms, but as a start toward building up a body of information. In Table 10 are shown the average R, A and D scores of groups of officers who occupy the same named positions in the same type of organization. Data are presented only for those groups which are represented by three or more officers in the same specialty in the same type of organization.

Inspection of Table 10 reveals rather marked differences among the various specialties. Those groups of officers who show the highest scores for *responsibility* are chief staff officers, supply officers and accounting officers of command staffs, training officers of a naval bureau, and training officers of naval shore stations. Commanding officers of submarines and destroyers rate themselves highest in *authority*. Those who describe themselves as *delegating* most authority to their immediate assistants are commanders of command staffs, and commanding officers of naval ships.

Use of the Scales

The RAD Scales were developed for experimental purposes. They should be used with caution by the practitioner.

It is believed that the scales have practical utility in gaining an increased understanding of responsibility-authority relationships among the members of organized groups. However, there is much experimental work to be done before any existing devices can be employed with confidence in the solution of day-to-day operating problems relative to responsibility and authority in military and industrial organizations. Use of the scales suggests that patterns of responsibility-authority relationships differ in large and small organizations. The results also suggest that in order to understand the authority-responsibility relationships exhibited by a given senior and his immediate juniors, it may be necessary to study the authority-responsibility-delegation pattern of a senior in a still higher echelon of the organization (or of juniors in lower echelons). Therefore, if it should be found in the study of a unit of organization that a particular senior is failing to delegate adequately to his juniors, the finding does not automatically imply the recommendation that the senior be instructed to give his juniors more authority. It might be well to determine whether the juniors are able or willing to carry out the responsibilities assigned to them, or whether the source of the difficulty might be located in a higher or lower echelon.

The patterns of relationships that operate in authority-responsibility interactions are of such a complex and obscure nature that they are not readily detected by direct observation. Therefore, instruments such as the RAD Scales can be of considerable value in building a body of information which will aid in a better understanding of the operations of organized groups.

THE RAD SCALES

A copy of the RAD Scales is shown on the pages immediately following. It will be noted that complete directions for using the scales are printed on the form.

THE RAD SCALES
THE OHIO STATE UNIVERSITY
Personnel Research Board

Leadership Studies

Name...

Position... Date.......................

Directions: Below are six separate scales. Two of these scales describe different degrees of *responsibility*. Two describe different degrees of *authority*, and two describe different degrees of *authority delegated to assistants and subordinates*.

For each scale please: *double check* ($\sqrt{}\sqrt{}$) the single statement which most accurately describes your status and practices in carrying out your duties, and *check* ($\sqrt{}$) the next most descriptive statement.

Double check ($\sqrt{}\sqrt{}$) = most descriptive statement

Check ($\sqrt{}$) = next most descriptive statement

Check only two items in each scale.

Scale I

( ) 1. I am responsible for the formulation and adoption of long range plans and policies.

( ) 2. I am responsible for making decisions which define operating policies.

( ) 3. My superior gives me a general idea of what he wants done. It is my job to decide how it shall be done and to see that it gets done.

( ) 4. It is my responsibility to supervise the work performed by my assistants and subordinates.

( ) 5. The operations of my unit are planned by my superiors. It is my responsibility to see that the plan is executed.

( ) 6. It is my responsibility to carry out direct orders which I received from my superior officers.

( ) 7. My responsibilities and duties are assigned daily in the form of specific tasks.

( ) 8. My superior approves each task I complete before I am permitted to undertake another.

Scale II

( ) 1. I have complete authority for establishing policies and goals of a general scope and establishing the lines of organizational authority and responsibility for the attainment of these goals.

( ) 2. I am authorized to make all decisions necessary for the implementation of long range plans.

( ) 3. In the main I can make and carry out all decisions which fall within the realm of established policy without consulting my superior or obtaining his approval.

( ) 4. I have complete authority on routine matters but refer the majority of unusual items to my superior for approval.

( ) 5. All questions of policy must be referred to my superior for his decision.

( ) 6. I frequently refer questions to my superior before taking any action.

( ) 7. I seldom make decisions or take action without approval from my superior.

( ) 8. My work procedures are fully outlined and allow little freedom in making decisions.

Scale III

( ) 1. My assistants have been granted authority to fulfill their duties in any manner they deem advisable.

( ) 2. My assistants have full authority, except that I retain the right to approve or disapprove of decisions affecting policy making.

( ) 3. My assistants have been authorized to make decisions on problems as they arise, but must keep me informed on matters of importance.

( ) 4. My assistants have authority to handle all routine matters in day-to-day operations.

( ) 5. My assistants may act in most routine matters.

( ) 6. Many of the responsibilities of my office cannot be entrusted to assistants.

( ) 7. My assistants have no actual authority to take action, but make recommendations regarding specific action to me.

( ) 8. I dictate detailed orders to my subordinates which they must carry out exactly as I specify, consulting me frequently if they are in doubt.

Scale IV

( ) 1. I am responsible for decisions relative to changes in long term policy.

( ) 2. I am responsible for making decisions relative to methods for effecting major changes in operations.

( ) 3. My superior always informs me as to the tasks to be performed and I am solely responsible for deciding how to fulfill these tasks and supervising their performance.

( ) 4. It is my responsibility to supervise the carrying out of orders which I receive from my superior.

( ) 5. I am responsible for making decisions relative to routine operations.

( ) 6. I execute direct orders given me by my superiors.

( ) 7. I have only my own routine tasks to account for.

( ) 8. I am not responsible for making decisions.

Scale V

( ) 1. I have completed authority for formulating policies of general nature and scope and for establishing lines of the entire organizational authority and responsibility.

( ) 2. I am authorized to make decisions which put all major plans and policies into action.

( ) 3. I refer only matters of an exceptional nature to my superior for approval. I settle most problems myself.

( ) 4. In situations not covered by instruction, I decide whether action is to be taken and what action to take.

( ) 5. I have no authority to act in matters where policy is not clearly defined.

( ) 6. I have authority to make decisions only as they are related to my own routine tasks.

( ) 7. I make decisions only when given explicit authority.

( ) 8. I follow a work schedule laid out for me by my superiors and have little authority to make changes.

Scale VI

( ) 1. I make decisions only when consulted in unusual circumstances, authorizing my assistants to exercise a high degree of authority and responsibility in making decisions.

( ) 2. I have delegated full authority to my assistants, other than the rights to prescribe policy and pass upon broad procedures.

( ) 3. I give my assistants a general idea of what I want done. It is their responsibility to decide how it shall be done and to see that it gets done.

( ) 4. I have delegated to my assistants authority to make all routine daily decisions.

( ) 5. I make most decisions coming within my scope of authority, although my assistants assume considerable responsibility for making decisions in routine matters where policies and procedures are well established.

( ) 6. I supervise my assistants fairly closely in their exercise of authority.

( ) 7. I make all important decisions coming within my scope of authority. My assistants are responsible for making decisions only in minor matters.

( ) 8. I have not found it advisable to delegate authority to my assistants.

VI

WORK ANALYSIS FORMS

The Work Analysis Forms were designed to measure various aspects of administrative performance. They represent a modified form of job analysis. The forms may be used by a subject for recording his estimates of the amount of time he spends in various kinds of work, or they may be used by an observer to record his estimates of another person's work.

DEVELOPMENT AND USE OF THE FORMS

Selecting Items for the Work Analysis Forms

The items for the Work Analysis Forms were derived empirically as a result of studying 6 business organizations and 14 military organizations. Interview data were used as sources of items descriptive of different kinds of executive duties and work performances. These items were used in a number of experimental forms for the study of business and military organizations. In the earliest forms, the subjects were asked to estimate the amount of time (in hours or minutes) spent in various kinds of work. In addition to the list of items, several spaces were provided for "other kinds of work." Analysis of the data recorded in these spaces revealed that business executives and navy officers were acutely conscious, not only of their responsibilities, but also of the "mechanics" of getting work done. Large amounts of time were recorded under such headings as "paper work," "reading and answering mail," "consulting assistants," and the like. As a result, the list of items was expanded, and was divided into three sections as follows:

A. Time spent in contacts with other persons.
B. Time spent in individual effort.
C. Time spent in major responsibilities.

The basis of estimating time was changed from an hourly to a percentage basis, in order to overcome the disadvantage connected with differences in the length of working days from one organization to another and from one time to another.

The subjects were also asked to make their estimates on the basis of a month, rather than on the basis of a single day, in order to obtain a more representative estimate of their work.

Data obtained from the study of 4 business and 16 navy organizations were used as a basis for making 8 separate revisions of the forms. Although subjects occasionally pointed out the fact that there is some overlap between the items in the final forms, they seldom found it necessary to write additional items in the spaces provided for "other kinds of work."

It has been found that variables which represent specific manipulative performances (such as using a pen or pencil, using calculating machines, using slide rules, and the like) do not give an adequate or representative account of administrative work. Some students of business organization, as represented by Davis,[1] maintain that the primary functions of executive leadership are the *planning, organizing* and *controlling* of the activities of organization. These variables are very general in nature, and would appear to be quite complex in structure. When measurements are made on variables that are complex in structure, there is a possibility that important differences between persons will be obscured because the sub-elements of the variables may tend to cancel each other. While it is desirable to avoid this cancelling effect insofar as possible, it seems necessary to describe administrative work in rather broad, general terms if realistic results are to be obtained.

Reliability of Work Analysis Forms

The Work Analysis Forms were administered to 32 officers in a Naval District Command Staff. One month later, the forms were administered again to the same officers. The correlations between the scores obtained in the first study and those obtained in the second study are shown in Table 11.

The test-retest correlations of items which describe work with other persons are higher, on the average, than those that describe individual effort or major responsibilities.

[1] Davis, Ralph C. *Industrial Organization and Management.* (New York: Harper, 1940).

TABLE 11—Correlation of First Score with Second Score on
Work Analysis Forms

(N = 32 Navy Officers)

Item No.	Item	r.
	Per Cent of Time Spent in Work with Persons	
12	Contacts with Persons (total time)	.57
13	Attending Conferences	.33
14	Consultation with Seniors	.43
15	Consultation with Peers	**.80**
16	Consultation with Juniors	.65
17	Consultation with Outside Persons	.68
18	Interviewing Personnel	.63
19	Making Speeches within Organization	.64
20	Making Speeches outside Organization	.41
21	Attending Meetings outside Organization	.52
22	Classroom Teaching and Instruction	.81
	Per Cent of Time Spent in Individual Effort	
11	Individual Effort (total time)	.57
23	Observation	.18
24	Reading and Answering Mail	.36
25	Examining Reports	.57
26	Writing Reports	.66
27	Reading Technical Publications	.28
28	Writing for Publication	.59
29	Reflection	.73
30	Mathematical Computation	.62
31	Preparing Charts	.43
32	Use of Instruments and Machines	.67
	Per Cent of Time Spent in Major Responsibilities	
33	Inspection	.51
34	Research	.59
35	Planning	.49
36	Preparing Procedures	.55
37	Coordination	.60
38	Evaluation	.58
39	Interpretation	.18
40	Supervision	.03
41	Personnel Functions	.46
42	Public Relations	.83
43	Professional Consultation	.61
44	Negotiations	.83
45	Scheduling, Routing	.38
46	Technical and Professional Performance	.59

The test-retest correlations are below .40 for such items as
attending conferences, observation, reading and answering mail,
reading technical publications, interpretation, supervision, and

scheduling. The correlations are higher than .70 for such items as consulting peers, teaching, reflection, public relations, and negotiations.

Two important factors must be taken into account in the interpretation of these results. The first is the fact that the tasks and operations of the organization may have changed during the interval of time between the two studies. Organization change would tend to lower the correlations. The second is the fact that test-retest correlations of scores derived from single items are usually found to be markedly lower than those of scores which consist of the sums of a large number of items. No method has been discovered for summing the items in the work analysis forms so as to derive a single meaningful score.

Validity

In the study of a Naval Air Station, 34 officers kept a log of work performance for a period of three days. The logs were col-

TABLE 12—Correlation Between Logged Time
and Estimated Time

Variable	r
Conversing with other persons (face to face and telephone)	.48
Attending meetings	.86
Classroom teaching	—.05
Observation	.52
Reading and answering mail	.62
Reading reports	.41
Writing reports	.66
Planning	—.02
Reflection	—.27
Research and investigation	—.11
Operating machines (e.g., flying planes)	.48

lected, and several days later the officers made estimates of the amount of time they had spent in various kinds of work during the period covered by the log. The correlations between logged time and estimated time are shown in Table 12.

The results suggest that there is a fairly high degree of correspondence between logged time and estimated time for objectively observable performances such as talking with other persons, reading and answering mail, reading and writing reports, and operating machines. Low correlations are obtained for those kinds of work for which very small amounts of time were logged or estimated. Classroom teaching and research are examples of this effect. More subjective, less readily observable performances, such as planning and reflection are not estimated in terms that correspond highly with time recorded on the log. A number of officers, when interviewed regarding this phenomenon, expressed the feeling that their estimates of time spent in planning were more accurate than the log, for the reason that they were not always aware at the moment that what they were doing constituted planning.

It is difficult, while conducting pressing business matters, to hunt out relevant items in a long list. In order to avert this difficulty, a random selection of items from the total list was employed.

In view of the many obstacles encountered, the results can hardly be regarded as indicative of the true validity of the work performance items.

Administration and Scoring

The Work Analysis Forms are self-administering questionnaires. Complete directions are contained on the forms. No additional instructions are required, except perhaps the suggestion that the subject check to make sure that his estimates add up to 100 per cent for each section of the test.

No scoring key is required. A subject's estimate of the per cent of time spent in a given kind of work is his score for that item.

Norms

There are no norms for the Work Analysis Forms. Although the research has revealed similar patterns of performance among groups of persons occupying similar positions in different organizations, there is also considerable variation among the individual members of these groups. For some types of positions, performance in large organizations is found to differ from that in small organizations. Performance also varies with changes in task requirements. For these reasons, it would be unwise to set up any arbitrary standards relative to the optimum distribution of working time in administrative positions.

CHART 4. Average Per Cent of Time Spent by 470 Navy Officers and
66 Business Executives in Different Kinds of Work

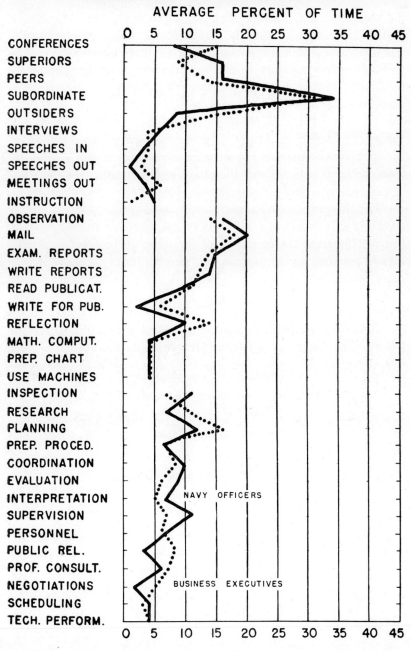

Chart 4 shows the profiles of average scores of 470 Navy officers and 66 business executives. The Navy sample includes officers from the top seven echelons of their organizations. The business executives are drawn from the top three echelons of a group of wholesale cooperative organizations. The differences in the profiles probably reflect variance in the performance characteristics of the two types of organizations, as well as differences in sampling procedures.

Use of the Forms

The Work Analysis Forms were devised for research purposes. However, it is believed that they have practical utility for the study of personal as well as organizational performance.

For the purposes of administrators who might wish to use the forms, it is believed that a profile of the scores of individuals will provide the most useful record of the data. A profile of scores is easy to prepare, is easy to read, and may be readily compared with other profiles.

WORK ANALYSIS FORM

A copy of the work analysis form is shown on the pages that follow. The directions for its use are printed on the form.

WORK ANALYSIS FORM
THE OHIO STATE UNIVERSITY
Personnel Research Board

Leadership Studies

Name..

Methods of Discharging Responsibilities

The purpose of this analysis is to determine the relative proportion of time spent in the utilization of various methods of getting work done.

Please consider your entire range of duties from day to day during the past month. Attempt to account for as much of your time as possible in terms of: (a) time spent in various types of contacts with persons, and (b) time spent in various types of individual effort. Before each item, please write the percentage of time spent in the work method described.

(%) A. Per cent of time spent in contacts with persons.

(%) B. Per cent of time spent in individual effort.

(100%) C. Total time spent in getting work done.

In parts A and B below, it is requested that you account in greater detail for your time spent in these two types of work methods.

A. *Time spent in contacts with persons:* (including committee meetings, interviews, telephone conversations, liaison, making speeches, meeting with outside groups, as well as face to face contacts).

Please account below for 100% of your time spent with persons. In the space before each item, please write the approximate percentage of time spent in the work method described.

(%) 1. Attending committee meetings and conferences (with self or other person acting as chairman)

(%) 2. Consulting with superior officers.

(%) 3. Consulting with associates at same echelon.

(%) 4. Consulting with assistants and subordinates.

(%) 5. Consulting with outside persons.

(%) 6. Interviewing personnel, applicants, etc.

(%) 7. Making speeches within the organization.

(%) 8. Making speeches to outside groups.

(%) 9. Attending meetings of outside groups.

(%) 10. Teaching, classroom instruction.

(%) 11. Other: ....

(100%)   Total time spent in contacts with persons.

B. *Time spent in individual effort:* (including personal observation, reading, thinking, computation, writing, dictation, use of instruments, forms and equipment).

Please account below for 100% of your time spent in individual effort.

(%) 1. Observation.

(%) 2. Reading and answering mail.

(%) 3. Examining reports (including correspondence prepared by others).

(%) 4. Preparing and writing reports.

(%) 5. Reading technical publications.

(%) 6. Writing for publication.

(%) 7. Thinking and reflection.

(%) 8. Mathematical computation.

(%) 9. Preparing charts, tables and diagrams.

(%) 10. Operation or use of instruments, machines, charts, examination forms.

(%) 11. Other: ....

(100%)   Total time spent in individual effort.

C. *Proportion of time devoted to major responsibilities.*

The purpose of this analysis is to determine the relative proportion of your time devoted to major administrative and operative responsibilities, disregarding the methods of accomplishment.

Please consider your entire range of responsibilities from day to day. Attempt to account as accurately as possible for the relative percentage of time devoted to various administrative and technical functions.

Before each item below, please write the approximate percentage of time spent in the responsibility described.

(%)   1. *Inspection of the Organization*—Direct observation and personal inspection of installations, buildings, equipment, facilities, operations, services or personnel—for the purpose of determining conditions and keeping informed.

(%)   2. *Investigation and Research*—Acts involving the accumulation and preparation of information and data. (Usually prepared and presented in the form of written reports.)

(%)   3. *Planning*—Preparing for and making decisions which will affect the aims or future activities of the organization as to volume or quality of business or service. (Including thinking, reflection and reading, as well as consultations and conferences with persons relative to short term and long range plans.)

(%)   4. *Preparation of Procedures and Methods*—Acts involving the mapping of procedures and methods for putting new plans into effect, as well as devising new methods for the performance of operations under existing plans.

(%)   5. *Coordination*—Acts and decisions designed to integrate and coordinate the activities of units within the organization or of persons within units, so as to achieve the maximal over-all efficiency, economy and control of operations.

(%)   6. *Evaluation*—Acts involving the consideration and evaluation of reports, corespondence, data, plans, divisions, or performances in relation to the aims, policies and standards of the organization.

(%)   7. *Interpretation of Plans and Procedures*—Acts involving the interpretation and clarification for assistants and other personnel of directives, regulations, practices and procedures.

(%)   8. *Supervision of Technical Operations*—Acts involving the direct supervision of personnel in the performance of duties.

(%)   9. *Personnel Activities*—Acts involving the selection, training, evaluation, motivation or disciplining of individuals, as well as acts designed to affect the morale, motivation, loyalty or harmonious cooperation of personnel.

(%) 10. *Public Relations*—Acts designed to inform outside persons, regarding the program and functions of the organization, to obtain information regarding public sentiment, or to create a favorable attitude toward the organization.

(%) 11. *Professional Consultation*—Giving professional advice and specialized assistance on problems of a specific or technical nature to persons within or outside the organization. (Other than technical supervision and guidance of own staff personnel.)

(%) 12. *Negotiations*—Purchasing, selling, negotiating contracts or agreements, settling claims, etc.

(%) 13. *Scheduling, Routing and Dispatching*—Initiating action and determining the time, place and sequence of operations.

(%) 14. *Technical and Professional Operations*—The performance of duties specific to a specialized profession (e.g., practice of medicine, conducting religious services, classroom teaching, auditing records, operating machines or equipment.)

(100%) Total time spent in major responsibilities.

VII

LEADER BEHAVIOR DESCRIPTIONS

The description of behavior and the evaluation of behavior are not identical processes. Most studies of leadership seek to evaluate behavior, no matter how varied the behavior of different persons may be, in terms of its effectiveness or ineffectiveness. In a logical order of procedures, it would seem that description should precede evaluation. The Leader Behavior Descriptions were developed for the purpose of describing behavior objectively in terms of its frequency of occurrence. The descriptive items can be used by a subject to describe his own behavior, or they can be used by one or more observers to describe the behavior of another person.

DEVELOPMENT AND USE OF LEADER BEHAVIOR DESCRIPTIONS

Development of the Descriptive Items

The Leader Behavior Descriptions were developed by staff members of the Ohio State Leadership Studies. An attempt was made to develop items which would represent 10 independent dimensions of observable behavior. This result was only partially achieved. The items were found to be rather highly intercorrelated.

A small number of highly selected items was used in the study of business and military organizations. The hypothetical dimensions selected for use were as follows:

> **Communication**—Six items descriptive of communicative behavior.
> **(Items 1, 11, 21, 31, 41 and 51 on Leader Behavior Form)**
>
> **Representation**—Four items descriptive of speaking and acting in behalf of the group.
> **(Items 2, 12, 22 and 32 on Leader Behavior Form)**
>
> **Organization**—Four items descriptive of behavior which prescribes ways of doing things.
> **(Items 3, 13, 23 and 33 on Leader Behavior Form)**
>
> **Integration**—Four items descriptive of behavior which tends to hold the group together as a working unit.
> **(Items 4, 14, 24 and 34 on Leader Behavior Form)**

The following items were added to the original list:

Relations with Subordinates—Two items descriptive of cordial relations with subordinates.
(Items 35 and 55 on Leader Behavior Form)
Relations with Superiors—Two items descriptive of cordial relations with superiors.
(Items 36 and 56 on Leader Behavior Form)

TABLE 13—Frequency Distributions of Descriptions of 48 Officers as Described by Themselves and as Described by 40 Peers

Item Number[a]	Type of Behavior	Described by Self						Described by Others					
		Response:						Response:					
		A	B	C	D	E	O	A	B	C	D	E	O
		Frequency of Response						Frequency of Response					
1	Communication	31	17					18	20	2			
11	Communication	15	26	7				11	22	6		1	
21	Communication	21	23	4				12	14	10	4		
31	Communication	27	19	1			1	19	17	4			
41	Communication	37	7	3		1		20	15	4		1	
51	Communication	24	23	1				13	21	5	1		
2	Representation	2	22	16	3	3	2	5	20	11	4		
12	Representation	10	9	16	5	8		8	12	9	4	5	2
22	Representation	6	8	9	13	12		4	3	14	9	6	4
32	Representation	32	12	4				19	18	2	1		
3	Organization	9	29	5	4		1	14	23	3			
13	Organization	30	13	5				22	12	5	1		
23	Organization	16	29	3				15	21	4			
33	Organization	31	14	2		1		17	19	3	1		
4	Integration	14	13	15	6			7	15	14	4		
14	Integration	28	20					19	12	6	1	1	1
24	Integration	33	13	2				18	18	4			
34	Integration	14	27	6		1		16	19	4	1		
35	Subordinates	21	20	7				19	17	3	1		
55	Subordinates	25	22	1				19	9	12			
36	Superiors	25	18	4	1			22	15	2			1
56	Superiors	27	18	3				19	17	3			1

Code: A=Always; B=Often; C=Occasionally; D=Seldom; E=Never; O=Omitted.
[a] For content of the items, see the Leader Behavior Description Scales.

These items were selected on the basis of the following criteria:

Contributions to high odd-even reliability of the total scale.
Contribution to the internal consistency of the scale.
Contribution to low inter-scale correlation.
Contribution to low correlation with a criterion of "good" leadership.

Appropriateness of the items for use in business and military organizations.

An extension of these criteria also determined the selection of the hypothetical dimensions or scales. An attempt was made to select items and scales which would describe behavior, but not evaluate behavior.

In Table 13 are shown the frequency distributions of the responses of 48 officers in a landing ship (LST) squadron who described their own behavior. Forty-two of these officers were also described, each by a single peer selected at random. It will be observed that when officers describe their own behavior the A (Always) category is used somewhat more frequently than when their behavior is described by peers.

Reliability

The best evidence of the reliability of the Leader Behavior Descriptions is provided by the results obtained in a naval district command staff which was studied on two separate occasions, with one month intervening between the two studies. The test-retest correlations obtained from this organization are shown in Table 14. Also shown in this table are the correlations between the odd items and the even items for each scale or hypothesized dimension. It will be observed that all the test-retest correlations as well as most of the

TABLE 14—Reliability of the Leader Behavior Descriptions

Dimension	Odd-Even Correlations			Test-Retest	Two Observers
	LST Squadron		District Staff	District Staff	Research Staff
	Self	Others[a]	Self	Self	Others[b]
	Correlation Coefficients				
Communication	.76	.85	.34	.70	.37
Representation	.67	.66	.57	.60	.33
Organization	.31	.75	.45	.67	.34
Integration	.56	.53	.66	.79	.44
Subordinates	.50	.51	.62	.52	.36
Superiors	.61	.55	.31	.74	.04
Total	.93	.89	.83	.82	.39
Number	**48**	**42**	**34**	**32**	**32**

[a] N = 42 Officers, each described by a single peer.
[b] N = 32 Superiors, each described by two subordinates.

odd-even correlations are above .50. The odd-even reliabilities are about as high as can be expected for scores based upon one to three items.

The correlations between the scores of two observers describing the same senior are also shown on Table 14. These correlations range from .04 to .44. It is apparent that these pairs of juniors are not in agreement when describing their immediate seniors' relationships with their seniors. They are in closer agreement when describing their seniors' integrative behavior, but none of the correlations indicates a high order of agreement.

Validity

No claims are made for the validity of the Leader Behavior Descriptions. When an individual describes his own behavior and is

TABLE 15—Correlation of Self-Descriptions with Descriptions by Others

Scale	Air Station	Submarines	Self vs Subordinates
	Self vs Superiors	Self vs Subordinates	Research Staff
	r.	r.	r.
Communication	.34	.21	.09
Organization	—.07	.18	.11
Integration	—.03	.17	.24
Representation	.16	.15	.05
Subordinates	.15	.31	.40
Superiors	. .	. .	.36
Number	45	69	47

also described by an observer, which description is the more accurate? The correlations between self-descriptions and descriptions by others are shown in Table 15. It is apparent from the results shown in this table that self-descriptions and descriptions by others are not in close agreement. This does not necessarily argue against the validity of self-descriptions. Research results have shown that subordinates who are not performing up to their own expectations tend to describe their superiors in less favorable terms, suggesting that descriptions by "others" need to be interpreted with as much caution as self-descriptions.

The correlations between the Leader Behavior Descriptions and other variables which might be regarded as criteria of "goodness" of leadership are shown in Table 16. Self-descriptions of leader be-

TABLE 16—Correlation of Leader Behavior Description Scores with Level in the Organization, Leadership Ratings by Superiors and Nominations for Best Leader by Subordinates

Scale	Described By	Level in Organization		Leadership Rating		Nominations
		Submarines	Research Staff	Submarines	Research Staff	Submarines
		r	r	r	r	r
Communication	Self	.28	−.25	−.14	.13	.06
	Subordinates	.63	−.26	.18	.08	.58
Organization	Self	−.02	−.23	.01	.11	−.01
	Subordinates	.55	−.12	.34	.07	.49
Integration	Self	.02	−.08	.08	−.07	.21
	Subordinates	.63	−.20	.27	.21	.74
Representation	Self	.28	.19	−.01	−.18	.09
	Subordinates	.55	.22	.09	.04	.64
Relation to Subordinates	Self	.26	−.20	.25	.06	.32
	Subordinates	.67	−.13	.17	.05	.57
Relation to Superiors	Self	..	.02	..	.07	..
	Subordinates	..	−.01	..	.07	..
Number		69[a]	57[b]	69	57	69

[a] r = .24 is significant at the .05 level when N = 69.
[b] r = .29 is significant at the .05 level when N = 47.

havior are not highly correlated with any of the criterion scores. Descriptions of leader behavior by subordinates are rather highly correlated with level in the organization and with nominations for best leader by subordinates. That is, subordinates tend to describe in more favorable terms those who occupy higher level positions and those whom they nominate most frequently for best leader. This is especially true in submarines. In a research staff, leader behavior descriptions by both self and subordinates tend to correlate negatively with level. Ratings of leader effectiveness by superiors fail to show high correlations with leader behavior descriptions by self and by subordinates both in submarines and in a research staff. It is apparent that the Leader Behavior Descriptions cannot be used as substitutes for leadership ratings by superiors. Self-descriptions of leader behavior cannot be used safely as criterion measures. Descriptions of leader behavior by subordinates show more promise as criterion measures.

Norms

There are no norms for the Leader Behavior Descriptions. However, for purposes of references and interpretation of findings, a table of average scores is shown below. These are the average scores of groups of officers in different positions aboard ship. The ships include cruisers, destroyers, submarines and landing ships.

It may be seen in Table 17 that there are few marked differences in leader behavior self-description scores between officers in the different positions. Commanding officers are shown to speak and act more frequently as representatives of their organizations. Executive

TABLE 17—Average Leader-Behavior, Self-Description Scores of Navy Officers in Different Positions Aboard Ship

Variable	Average Leader-Behavior Score					
	Commanding Officers	Executive Officers	Operations Officers	Engineer Officers	Communications Officers	Supply Officers
Communication	7.3	7.1	7.2	7.3	7.0	7.0
Organization	6.3	6.5	6.3	6.7	6.0	6.6
Integration	6.5	6.6	6.5	6.3	6.4	6.5
Representation	5.2	4.9	4.8	4.1	4.6	5.0
Subordinates	6.0	6.0	5.4	5.1	5.0	5.0
Superiors	7.0	6.8	6.3	6.4	6.3	6.3
Number	**24**	**25**	**16**	**22**	**23**	**19**

officers obtain slightly higher scores on integrative behavior. Commanders and executive officers describe themselves as higher than other officers in maintaining cordial relations with both superiors and subordinates. Engineering officers, who direct large departments, obtain the highest average score in organizing behavior; while communications officers, who direct small departments, describe themselves as lowest on this variable. These results, although not statistically significant, appear to reflect meaningful differences in the functions of the several positions.

Administration and Scoring

The Leader Behavior Descriptions are self-administering. The directions are printed on the test forms.

The scoring key is the same for each item. The scoring key for each item is shown below:

Scoring Key

Response	Score
Always	4
Often	3
Occasionally	2
Seldom	1
Never	0

The score for any one scale or dimension is obtained by summing the scores of the items in that particular scale. The items contained in each scale are shown below:

Communication score is the sum of items   1, 11, 21, 31, 41, 51
Representation score is the sum of items   2, 12, 22, 32
Organization score is the sum of items   3, 13, 23, 33
Integration score is the sum of items   4, 14, 24, 34
Relations with subordinates is the sum of items 35, 55
Relations with superiors is the sum of items   36, 56
Total score is the sum of the scores of all the items.

Use of the Descriptions

The Leader Behavior Descriptions were devised for research purposes. The items, when used for self-descriptions, show low correlations with various criteria of "good" leadership and, for this reason, cannot be used as criteria of leadership quality. However, descriptions by subordinates have been shown to be meaningfully and differentially related to other measures of leader performance and organization structure.

LEADER BEHAVIOR DESCRIPTION SCALES

A copy of the leader behavior description scales is shown on the following pages. Directions for administration are printed on the form.

It has been demonstrated that extremely short scales for the description of leader behavior have some utility for research purposes. However, short scales are usually less reliable than is desired for practical use. Recently, two factored scales for the description of leader behavior have been prepared by the Ohio State Leadership Studies Staff. These scales, each composed of 15 items, are more reliable than the short scales described in this manual. It is anticipated that the factored scales will be made available in the near future. Their use, rather than the short scales, is recommended.

LEADER BEHAVIOR DESCRIPTION SCALES

THE OHIO STATE UNIVERSITY
Personnel Research Board

Leadership Studies

The questions which follow make it possible to describe objectively the behavior of individuals in leadership positions. The items simply describe the leader's behavior; they do not judge whether the behavior is desirable or undesirable. Therefore, in no way are the questions to be considered a "test" either of the ability of the persons answering the items or of the quality of the leader's behavior. We simply want an objective description of what leaders *actually do.*

> *Note:* The term, *"group,"* as employed in the following items, refers to a department, division, or other unit of organization which is supervised by the person being described. The term, *"members,"* refers to all personnel in the unit of organization which is supervised by the person being described.

Name of the person you are describing...

Name of the unit which he leads...

Your name...

DIRECTIONS:
1. READ each item carefully.
2. THINK about how frequently the leader engages in the behavior described by the item.

3. READ the five answers provided after the item and decide which one of the five most nearly expresses the frequency with which the leader engages in the behavior.

4. DRAW a line under the answer you have selected.

1. HE KEEPS INFORMED ABOUT THE WORK THAT IS BEING DONE.
A. always   B. often   C. occasionally   D. seldom   E. never

2. HE MAKES OUTSIDE CONTACTS FOR THE GROUP.
A. always   B. often   C. occasionally   D. seldom   E. never

3. HE SCHEDULES THE WORK TO BE DONE.
A. always   B. often   C. occasionally   D. seldom   E. never

4. HE WORKS RIGHT ALONG WITH THE GROUP.
A. always   B. often   C. occasionally   D. seldom   E. never

11. HE EXPLAINS WHY A PARTICULAR ACTION IS IMPORTANT.
A. always   B. often   C. occasionally   D. seldom   E. never

12. HE SELLS THE PUBLIC ON THE IMPORTANCE OF HIS GROUP.
A. always   B. often   C. occasionally   D. seldom   E. never

13. HE ASKS THAT MEMBERS FOLLOW ORGANIZATIONAL LINES.
A. always   B. often   C. occasionally   D. seldom   E. never

14. HE LOOKS OUT FOR THE WELFARE OF INDIVIDUAL MEMBERS.
A. always   B. often   C. occasionally   D. seldom   E. never

21. HE GIVES ADVANCE NOTICE OF CHANGES.
A. always   B. often   C. occasionally   D. seldom   E. never

22. HE SPEAKS IN PUBLIC IN THE NAME OF THE GROUP.
A. always   B. often   C. occasionally   D. seldom   E. never

23. HE FIGURES AHEAD ON WHAT SHOULD BE DONE.
A. always   B. often   C. occasionally   D. seldom   E. never

24. HE ENCOURAGES MEMBERS TO WORK AS A TEAM.
A. always   B. often   C. occasionally   D. seldom   E. never

31. HE KEEPS WELL INFORMED ABOUT THE PROGRESS OF THE GROUP.
A. always   B. often   C. occasionally   D. seldom   E. never

32. HE BACKS UP THE MEMBERS IN THEIR ACTIONS.
A. always   B. often   C. occasionally   D. seldom   E. never

33. HE ENCOURAGES THE USE OF CERTAIN UNIFORM PROCEDURES.
A. always   B. often   C. occasionally   D. seldom   E. never

34. HE MAKES IT PLEASANT TO BE A MEMBER OF THE GROUP.
A. always   B. often   C. occasionally   D. seldom   E. never

35. HE ESTABLISHES CORDIAL RELATIONS WITH
    SUBORDINATES.
    A. always   B. often   C. occasionally   D. seldom   E. never

36. HE ESTABLISHES CORDIAL RELATIONS WITH SUPERIORS.
    A. always   B. often   C. occasionally   D. seldom   E. never

41. HE KNOWS WHO IS RESPONSIBLE FOR EACH JOB.
    A. always   B. often   C. occasionally   D. seldom   E. never

51. HE KEEPS THE GROUP INFORMED.
    A. always   B. often   C. occasionally   D. seldom   E. never

55. HE MAINTAINS A CLOSE WORKING RELATIONSHIP WITH
    SUBORDINATES.
    A. always   B. often   C. occasionally   D. seldom   E. never

56. HE MAINTAINS A CLOSE WORKING RELATIONSHIP WITH
    SUPERIORS.
    A. always   B. often   C. occasionally   D. seldom   E. never

VIII

EFFECTIVENESS RATINGS

Effectiveness ratings are useful when it is desired to obtain judgments relative to "goodness" of performance. It is the aim of personnel selection procedures to obtain persons who will perform satisfactorily in the positions to which they are to be assigned. Promotions and salary increases are, in many organizations, based upon effectiveness of performance. In military organizations, where there are few objective criteria such as increases in production rates or volume of sales, it becomes necessary to rely upon human judgment in order to arrive at evaluations of performance. Much experimental work has demonstrated that such evaluations are likely to be made in "all" or "none" terms. If a person is rated as very good on one item he is also likely to be rated as very good on other items by the same rater. There has also been observed a tendency, especially in military organizations, for most persons to be rated toward the "very good" or "excellent" end of the scale. Few persons are rated as "average" or "below average." In order to overcome the latter difficulty, a rating scheme was employed which requires all the immediate subordinates being rated by a given superior to be ranked in order of merit. The same scheme was employed in obtaining effectiveness ratings of units of organization.

The Ranking-Rating Scales

Samples of two rating scales are shown at the end of this section. One is a form for obtaining ratings on leadership effectiveness. The other is a generalized rating scale which may be used for obtaining ratings of either persons or units of organizations on any observable performance or characteristic. Both of these forms involve a rank ordering of persons or units, combined with a rating of each person or unit in terms of "Poor," "Fair," "Good," or "Excellent." The scoring key for this rating-ranking method is also shown following the rating forms, and instructions for the use of the key accompany it.

Use of Effectiveness Ratings

It is very difficult to devise a rating scheme that is satisfactory for all the purposes for which effectiveness ratings may be desired. The rating scheme described in this section requires further research in order to obtain additional evidence relative to its reliability and validity.

The rating scales herein described should be of value when a normal distribution of ratings is desired. However, in order to obtain a normal distribution of ratings, it is necessary that each superior rate several (more than 4 or 5) subordinates, or that each superior rate an approximately equal number of subordinates.

The scales may be used for rating individuals, organizations or units of organization on various observable characteristics.

When the generalized effectiveness rating form is used it should be accompanied by a set of directions specifying whether persons, organizations or units of organization are to be rated, and defining the variables (trait or performance) on which they are to be rated. The Leadership Effectiveness Rating Form shows such a set of directions.

Reliability and Validity

In the study of a research organization, 57 officers were each rated by two seniors on military leadership. The seniors were randomly divided into two groups. The correlation between the ratings of the two sets of seniors is .46. The distributions of the two sets of ratings are shown in Table 18. It will be observed that the means of scores are centered around the midpoint of the scale, rather than being skewed toward the more favorable end of the scale. The correlation of .46 between the two sets of raters suggests that the raters were not in close agreement in their perception of the effectiveness of the subjects being rated.

One desirable feature of the rating-ranking scheme is that it results in a normal distribution of scores. It prevents the rating of all persons as being uniformly excellent. This is an advantage when it is desired to discriminate among the persons being rated, which is the aim of most rating systems.

No claims are made relative to the validity of the effectiveness

TABLE 18—Distribution of Leader-Effectiveness Ratings of 57 Officers Each Rated by Two Superiors

Score	Frequency	
	Group 1	Group 2
9	2	4
8	2	4
7	7	11
6	6	9
5	11	6
4	12	11
3	10	6
2	2	4
1	1	
0	4	2
Mean	**4.51**	**5.26**

TABLE 19—"Efficient Ship" Ratings Correlated with Other Variables: Rank Order Correlations

Other Variables	Correlation Coefficients	
	Efficient Ship Ratings:	
	By Officers	By Enlisted Men
1. "Happy Ship" Ratings by H. Q. Officers	.6	.5
2. "Happy Ship" Ratings by H. Q. Enlisted Men	.6	.7
3. Reenlistment Rate on Ship	.1	.2
4. Total Disciplinary Offenses	—.2	—.2
5. Torpedo Firing Accuracy	.6	.7

TABLE 20—Correlation of "Military Leadership" Ratings with Other Variables

Variables	Correlation Coefficients	
	Submarines	Research Staff
1. Military Rank	.16	.15
2. Level in Organization	.19	.14
3. Time in Position	.21	—.01
4. Nomination for Wartime Leader by Subordinates	.38[a]	
5. Fitness Reports—Present	.08	
6. Sociometric Score (Received)	.45[a]	.20
7. Unit Morale—Own Ship	.09	
8. Responsibility	.12	—.02
9. Authority	—.03	—.22
10. Delegation	.10	—.06
N	**69**	**57**

[a] Significant at the .01 level.

ratings. However, the ratings do show satisfactorily high correlations with other measures of unit effectiveness. For example, the rank order correlation of unit effectiveness ratings with other measures for ten ships is shown in Table 19. It will be seen that effectiveness ratings of the ships are correlated about .6 with morale (Happy Ship) ratings and with torpedo-accuracy scores. Those ships with better morale and higher torpedo accuracy scores are rated as more effective by headquarters staff officers.

In Table 20 are shown the correlations (Pearsonian) between military leadership ratings and other variables. The subjects are 69 commissioned officers in a squadron of submarines, and 57 officers and civilian administrators in a naval research organization. The subjects were rated by their immediate superiors. Two of the correlations for submarine officers are statistically significant. One is the correlation of .38 between superiors' ratings of the military leadership of the subjects and the number of nominations given them by subordinates for "Wartime Leader." The nominations were made by non-commissioned personnel, who listed the personnel on the ship whom they would prefer as commander of their ship under wartime conditions. The second is the correlation of .45 between military leadership ratings and number of mentions received as work partner. The mentions were made by all personnel aboard ship. There is observed a slight tendency for those who hold higher military rank and who occupy higher level positions to be rated higher in military leadership, but the correlations are not statistically significant. There is a slight tendency for those who rate themselves higher in authority to be rated lower in military leadership. The most significant results shown in Table 20 are the correlations of .38 and .45 which indicate that subordinates and superiors tend to agree in their estimates of the leadership ability of the persons being evaluated. These findings suggest that leadership rankings and ratings exhibit a moderate degree of validity for the evaluation of individual leadership ability. However, the results of Table 19 suggest that ratings of the effectiveness of units of organization show more promise as criterion measures than do ratings of individual leadership.

EFFECTIVENESS RATING FORMS AND SCORING KEY

Copies of the rating forms and of the scoring key are shown immediately following. The same scoring key is used for the generalized rating form and for the leadership effectiveness rating form. The generalized form should be accompanied by specific directions prepared to describe its intended use.

GENERALIZED EFFECTIVENESS RATING FORM

THE OHIO STATE UNIVERSITY
Personnel Research Board
Leadership Studies

RATING SHEET

Ratings of: ....

Ratings by: ....

Rated on:* ....

(LIST IN ORDER OF MERIT) *Names* (Persons or Units)*	(How Good? Poor	Fair	Good	Check One) Excellent
1. Best				
2. Next Best				
3. Next				
4. Next				
5. Next				
6. Next				
7. Next				
8. Next				
9. Next				
10. Next				

* *Note:* In preparing this form for use, a set of directions should be prepared specifying whether persons, organizations or units of organization are to be rated, and defining the variable on which they are to be rated. An example of such a set of directions is shown on the Leadership Effectiveness Rating Form.

LEADERSHIP EFFECTIVENESS RATING FORM

Name of person making ratings:..

Variable being rated: LEADERSHIP EFFECTIVENESS

We would like for you to evaluate the personnel who are under your immediate direction, in terms of their leadership effectiveness. Which ones are the best leaders?

On the first line, enter the name of the person whom you consider to be the best leader. List the remaining personnel under your direction in order of their merit as leaders. After each name, check one of the descriptive terms; Poor, Fair, Good, Excellent, to indicate how good a leader you regard him to be.

(LIST IN ORDER OF MERIT) Names of Persons	(HOW GOOD A LEADER? Poor	 Fair	 Good	CHECK ONE) Excellent
1. Best				
2. Next Best				
3. Next				
4. Next				
5. Next				
6. Next				
7. Next				
8. Next				
9. Next				
10. Next				

SCORING KEY FOR EFFECTIVENESS RATINGS

The scoring key for the effectiveness-rating forms is shown below.
Scoring Key for Effectiveness Ratings

(LIST IN ORDER OF MERIT) Names of Persons or Units	(HOW GOOD? Poor	 Fair	 Good	CHECK ONE) Excellent
1. Best	3	5	7	9
2. Next Best	2	4	6	8
3. Next	1	3	5	7
4. Next	0	2	4	6
5. Next	0	1	3	5
6. Next	0	0	2	4
7. Next	0	0	1	3
8. Next	0	0	0	2
9. Next	0	0	0	1
10. Next	0	0	0	0

How to Use the Scoring Key

If the person or unit ranked as first (best) is also checked as excellent, the score is shown to be 9. However, if the person ranked as first is checked as (good) he obtains a score of 7. If the person ranked as second (next best) is checked as excellent he obtains a score of 8, but his score will be 4 if he is checked as only fair. The fourth name on the list will receive a score of 6 if checked as excellent, but a score of 0 (zero) if checked as poor.

The same scoring key is used for the generalized effectiveness rating form and for the leadership effectiveness rating form.

IX

DISCUSSION

The methods described in this monograph were devised for research purposes. It was the primary aim of the research to produce theory, methodology and information which might serve as a basis for the development of improved and more effective techniques in the fields of organization analysis, position analysis and personnel placement.

The methods were designed for the study of organization in terms of the status, behavior and personal interactions of the members. The methods were used to provide a body of information relative to the characteristics of individuals, their jobs and their organization. Personnel evaluation, position analysis and organization analysis were combined to form an integrated body of procedures.

Should it be desired to use the methods described in this monograph as a basis for stimulating the invention and development of improved techniques, there are several cautions that should be kept in mind. The responses given by persons in a research setting may differ from those they might give if their future advancement or the advancement of their associates were dependent upon their answers. There are no norms available for determining a desirable or optimum score for individuals, jobs or organizations. The reliabilities of most of the forms need to be increased if they are to be used for predictive purposes.

It is recommended that the methods be used for research purposes only.

APPENDIX A

Monographs
in the
Leadership Series in Ohio Studies in Personnel
Published in Cooperation with
The Personnel Research Board

Bureau of Business Research Monographs

R–80   *Methods in the Study of Administrative Leadership,*
       by Ralph M. Stogdill and Carroll L. Shartle

   This monograph consists of a set of manuals which describe various methods that were developed for use in the Ohio State Leadership Studies. The methods include interviews, measures of organization structure, sociometric measures of personal interaction, measures of work performance, responsibility, authority, delegation and leader behavior, and ratings of effectiveness. Data on the reliability and validity of the various methods, and directions for administration and scoring of the various tests and scales are included.

R–81   *Patterns of Administrative Performance,*
       by Ralph M. Stogdill, Carroll L. Shartle and Associates

   The four studies included in this monograph attempt to answer questions concerning the relationship of performance to the type of position occupied by an administrator. The methods used for the collection of data are those described in Monograph No. R–80. The data are analyzed in terms of differences between persons, between types of positions, between types of organizations and between levels (status) in the organization hierarchy.

R–82   *Leadership and Perceptions of Organization,*
       by Ellis L. Scott

   In this study of enlisted men aboard submarines, each man's perception of the structure of his unit of organization was compared with an organization chart prepared for his unit. The data are analyzed in terms of (1) discrepancies between perceived organization and charted organization, and (2) correspondences (reciprocations) between the perceptions of superiors, peers and subordinates. The relationship of perceptual error and perceptual reciprocation to morale, unit effectiveness and other variables is discussed. The methods used are based, in part, on those described in Monograph No. R–80.

R–83   *Leadership and Its Effects Upon the Group,*
        by Donald T. Campbell

   This monograph, based on the study of a squadron of submarines, is concerned with the effects of leadership upon group performance and morale. A wide variety of criterion scores, including some 60 measures of effectiveness and morale for ships and for units of organization within ships, are analyzed and related to measures of leadership among commissioned and non-commissioned personnel. The criterion scores include objective measures as well as reputational data and evaluative ratings. The methods are based in part on those described in Monograph R–80.

R–84   *Leadership and Structures of Personal Interaction,*
        by Ralph M. Stogdill

   This monograph describes (1) a sociometric study of personal interaction in organizations of various sizes, and (2) a study of responsibility-authority relationships between superiors and subordinates in large and small organizations. Data on the relation of interaction measures and of responsibility and authority scores to measures of status, leader behavior and other variables are presented. Analysis of the data indicate that the performances, interactions, responsibility and authority of superiors exert a direct effect upon the performances and interactions of subordinates.

R–85   *A Predictive Study of Administrative Work Patterns,*
        by Ralph M. Stogdill, Carroll L. Shartle, Ellis L. Scott, Alvin E. Coons and William E. Jaynes

   Twenty navy officers were studied before being transferred to new positions. The twenty officers whom the transferees were to replace were also studied. The data obtained from the study of these two sets of officers were used to predict the future behavior of the officers being transferred. Six months later they were restudied on their new jobs. It was found that some forms of behavior were predicted more accurately in terms of the previous behavior of the men being transferred. Other behaviors were predicted more accurately in terms of the behavior of the previous occupants of the jobs. The methods for collecting data are described in Monograph No. R–80.

R–86   *Leadership and Role Expectations,*
        by Ralph M. Stogdill, Ellis L. Scott, and William E. Jaynes

   In this study of a large research organization, 57 civilian and military administrators were asked to describe what they do and what they ought to do on 45 items of work performance, leader behavior, responsibility and authority. The "does" and "ought to do" behaviors of each subject were also described by two subordinates. The data are analyzed in terms of relationships between expectations and performance, as well as in terms of discrepancies between expectations and performance. The methods for collecting data are described in Monograph R–80.

R–87   *Group Dimensions: A Manual for Their Measurement,*
         by John K. Hemphill

This monograph describes a set of scales for the measurement of thirteen different dimensions of social groups. Normative data derived from the study of a wide variety of groups, as well as data on the reliability and validity of the scales are presented. The instructions include directions for administration and scoring. Data on the relation of group dimension scores to measures of productivity and job satisfaction are presented.

R–88   *Leader Behavior: Its Description and Measurement,*
         by Ralph M. Stogdill and Alvin E. Coons, Editors

This monograph consists of a collection of papers by staff members of the Ohio State Leadership Studies. The papers describe the development, analysis and application of a set of items devised for the description of leader behavior. These items were used for the description of the leader behavior of business executives, foremen, teachers, college administrators, Air Force officers and Navy officers. Data on the relation of leader behavior to effectiveness measures, group descriptions and altitude climate are presented. A copy of the Leader Bahavior Descriptions Questionnaire and Directions for its use are also included.

Bureau of Educational Research Monographs

No–32   *Situational Factors in Leadership,*
            by John K. Hemphill, 1949, 140 pp.

This monograph presents the results obtained from a questionnaire study of 500 groups and their leaders. Each group was described by a member who checked scaled statements designed to describe 15 different group dimensions. The same member also described the behavior and evaluated the adequacy of the top leader of the group. The data are analyzed in terms of the interrelationships between leader behavior, leadership adequacy and group dimensions.

No–33   *Leadership and Supervision in Industry: An Evaluation of a*
            Supervisory Training Program,
               by Edwin A. Fleishman, Edwin F. Harris and Harold E. Burtt,
               1955, 110 pp.

This monograph describes a study designed to evaluate the results of a training program for foremen in a large manufacturing plant. The subjects were three matched groups of foremen who had completed the human relations training course at different times, and a matched group of untrained foremen. The subjects described their own attitudes about how groups should be supervised and also described the behavior of their own supervisors. The superior and the subordinates of each foreman also described the behavior of the foreman and indicated their conception of the behavior of an ideal foreman. The analysis compares trained and untrained foremen, and compares the behavior, attitudes and effectiveness of foremen who operate under different patterns of leadership.

APPENDIX B

Publications in Books and Journals
by
Members of the Staff of
The Ohio State Leadership Studies
Personnel Research Board

1. BASS, BERNARD M., An Analysis of the Leaderless Group Discussion. *Journal of Applied Psychology,* 1949, *33* (6), 527–533.

2. BROWNE, C. G., A Study of Executive Leadership in Business: I. The R, A, and D Scales. *Journal of Applied Psychology,* 1949, *33* (6), 521–526.

3. BROWNE, C. G., Study of Executive Leadership in Business: II. Social Group Patterns. *Journal of Applied Psychology,* 1950, *34* (1), 12–15.

4. BROWNE, C. G., Study of Executive Leadership in Business: III. Goal and Achievement Index. *Journal of Applied Psychology,* 1950, *34* (2), 82–87.

5. BROWNE, C. G., Study of Executive Leadership in Business: IV. Sociometric Pattern. *Journal of Applied Psychology,* 1951, *35* (1), 34–37.

6. CANTER, RALPH R., JR., A Human Relations Training Program. *Journal of Applied Psychology,* 1951, *35* (1), 38–45.

7. COONS, ALVIN E., *A Study of Organization, Division of Authority and Responsibility and Executive Compensation in Four Regional Cooperatives.* (Columbus: The Ohio State University Personnel Research Board, 1948). (Out of print technical report).

8. FLEISHMAN, EDWIN A., HARRIS, EDWIN F. AND BURTT, HAROLD E., *Leadership and Supervision in Industry: An Evaluation of a Supervisory Training Program.* (Columbus: The Ohio State University, Bureau of Educational Research Monograph No. 33, 1955).

9. FLEISHMAN, EDWIN A., Leadership Climate, Human Relations Training and Supervisory Behavior. *Personnel Psychology,* 1953, *6* (1), 205–222.

10. GEKOSKI, NORMAN, Group Characteristics and Industrial Productivity. *Engineering Experiment Station News,* 1952, *24* (5), 39–42.

11. HALPIN, ANDREW W., Current Conceptual Trends in Small Group Study: Social Psychology. *Autonomous Groups Bulletin,* 1952, *7* (2 & 3), 4–17.

12. HALPIN, ANDREW W., The Leadership Behavior and Combat Performance of Airplane Commanders. *Journal of Abnormal and Social Psychology,* 1954, *49* (1), 19–22.

13. HALPIN, ANDREW W., The Leadership Ideology of Aircraft Commanders. *Journal of Applied Psychology,* 1955, *39,* 82–84.

14. HARRIS, EDWIN F. AND FLEISHMAN, EDWIN A., Human Relations Training and the Stability of Leadership Patterns. *Journal of Applied Psychology,* 1955, *39,* 20–25.

15. HEMPHILL, JOHN K., Group Factors in Leadership: Relations between the Size of the Group and the Behavior of Superior Leaders. *Journal of Social Psychology,* 1950, *32,* 11–22.

16. HEMPHILL, JOHN K. AND WESTIE, CHARLES M., The Measurement of Group Dimensions. *Journal of Psychology,* 1950, *29,* 325–342.

17. HEMPHILL, JOHN K., *Leader Behavior Description.* 1950. (Ohio State Leadership Studies staff report).

18. HEMPHILL, JOHN K., *Situational Factors in Leadership.* (Columbus: The Ohio State University, Bureau of Educational Research Monograph No. 32, 1950).

19. HEMPHILL, JOHN K., AND SECHREST, LEE B., A Comparison of Three Criteria of Aircrew Effectiveness in Combat Over Korea. *Journal of Applied Psychology,* 1952, *36* (5), 323–327.

20. HITES, R. W., *Personal and Social Adjustment in Industry:* An outline of suggested problems and methods of research. (Columbus: The Ohio State University, Bureau of Business Research, Ohio Studies in Personnel, Research Monograph No. 60, 1950).

21. MORRIS, RICHARD T., AND SEEMAN, MELVIN, The Problem of Leadership: An Interdisciplinary Approach. *The American Journal of Sociology,* 1950, *56* (2), 149–155.

22. SEEMAN, MELVIN, Some Status Correlates of Leadership. In *Leadership in American Education,* Vol. III, pages 40–50. Proceedings of the Cooperative Conference for Administrative Officers of Public and Private Schools, Northwestern University and the University of Chicago. Edited by Alonzo G. Grace. (Chicago: University of Chicago Press, 1950).

23. SEEMAN, MELVIN, Role Conflict and Ambivalence in Leadership. *American Journal of Sociology,* 1953, *18* (4), 373–380.

24. SHARTLE, CARROLL L., Leadership and Executive Performance. *Personnel,* 1949, *25,* 370–380.

25. SHARTLE, CARROLL L., Organization Structure. In *Current Trends in Industrial Psychology.* (Pittsburgh: University of Pittsburgh Press, 1949).

26. SHARTLE, CARROLL L., Studies of Leadership by Interdisciplinary Methods. In *Leadership in American Education,* Vol. III. Proceedings of the Cooperative Conference for Administrative Officers of Public and Private Schools, University of Chicago and Northwestern University. Edited by Alonzo G. Grace. (Chicago: University of Chicago Press, 1950).

27. SHARTLE, CARROLL L., Leadership Aspects of Administrative Behavior. *Advanced Management,* 1950, *15* (11), 12–15.

28. SHARTLE, CARROLL L., Studies in Naval Leadership, Part I. In *Groups, Leadership and Men: Research in Human Relations*. H. Guetzkow, editor. (Pittsburgh: Carnegie Press, 1951).

29. SHARTLE, CARROLL L., Leader Behavior in Jobs. *Occupations*, 1951, *30* (3), 164–166.

30. SHARTLE, CARROLL L., Ohio State Leadership Studies. *The Ohio State University, Engineering Experiment Station News*, 1952, *24* (5), 16–21.

31. STODGILL, RALPH M. AND SHARTLE, CARROLL L., Methods for Determining Patterns of Leadership Behavior in Relation to Organization Structure and Objectives. *Journal of Applied Psychology*, 1948, *32*, 286–291.

32. STOGDILL, RALPH M., Personal Factors Associated with Leadership: A Survey of the Literature. *Journal of Psychology*, 1948, *25*, 35–71.

33. STOGDILL, RALPH M., Leadership, Membership, and Organization. *Psychological Bulletin*, 1950, *47* (1), 1–14.

34. STOGDILL, RALPH M., The Organization of Working Relationships: Twenty Sociometric Indices. *Sociometry*, 1951, *14*, 366–374.

35. STOGDILL, RALPH M., Studies in Naval Leadership, Part II. In *Groups, Leadership and Men: Research in Human Relations*. H. Guetzkow, editor. (Pittsburgh: Carnegie Press, 1951).